50 Holiday Baking Tradition Recipes for Home

By: Kelly Johnson

Table of Contents

- Classic Sugar Cookies
- Gingerbread Cookies
- Peppermint Bark
- Pecan Pie Bars
- Chocolate Fudge
- Linzer Cookies
- Rum Balls
- Eggnog Cheesecake
- Stollen (German Christmas bread)
- Yule Log Cake (Bûche de Noël)
- Rugelach
- Panettone
- Cranberry Orange Scones
- Snowball Cookies (Russian Tea Cakes)
- Holiday Fruitcake
- Candy Cane Macarons
- Almond Biscotti
- Cinnamon Rolls
- Pumpkin Pie
- Mince Pies
- Red Velvet Cupcakes
- Danish Butter Cookies
- Hot Cross Buns
- Lebkuchen (German spiced cookies)
- Chocolate Peppermint Bark Cookies
- Coconut Macaroons
- Cranberry Pistachio Biscotti
- Snowflake Shortbread Cookies
- Caramel Pecan Turtle Clusters
- Chocolate Covered Pretzels
- Cinnamon Sugar Palmiers
- Lemon Bars
- Chocolate Truffles
- Holiday Thumbprint Cookies
- Cherry Almond Bread

- Irish Cream Brownies
- Candy Cane Marshmallow Pops
- Cranberry Bliss Bars
- Apricot Rugelach
- Maple Pecan Pie
- Spiced Apple Pie
- Peppermint Mocha Cupcakes
- Caramel Apple Tart
- White Chocolate Peppermint Fudge
- Ginger Snaps
- Chocolate-Dipped Madeleines
- Pistachio Cranberry Biscotti
- Nutella Swirl Bread
- Eggnog Bread Pudding
- Sparkling Cranberry Orange Cookies

Classic Sugar Cookies

Ingredients:

- 2 3/4 cups all-purpose flour
- 1 teaspoon baking powder
- 1/2 teaspoon salt
- 1 cup unsalted butter, softened
- 1 1/2 cups granulated sugar
- 1 large egg
- 2 teaspoons vanilla extract

Instructions:

1. Preheat Oven: Preheat your oven to 350°F (175°C) and line baking sheets with parchment paper.
2. Mix Dry Ingredients: In a medium bowl, whisk together the flour, baking powder, and salt. Set aside.
3. Cream Butter and Sugar: In a large mixing bowl, beat the softened butter and granulated sugar together until light and fluffy, about 2-3 minutes.
4. Add Egg and Vanilla: Beat in the egg and vanilla extract until well combined.
5. Incorporate Dry Ingredients: Gradually add the flour mixture to the wet ingredients, mixing until the dough comes together and there are no streaks of flour. Be careful not to overmix.
6. Chill Dough (Optional): If the dough is too soft, you can chill it in the refrigerator for about 30 minutes to make it easier to roll out.
7. Roll and Cut: On a lightly floured surface, roll out the dough to about 1/4-inch thickness. Use cookie cutters to cut out desired shapes.
8. Bake: Place the cut-out cookies on the prepared baking sheets, spacing them about 1 inch apart. Bake in the preheated oven for 8-10 minutes or until the edges are just beginning to turn golden.
9. Cool and Decorate: Remove from the oven and let the cookies cool on the baking sheets for a few minutes before transferring to a wire rack to cool completely. Once cooled, decorate with icing, sprinkles, or colored sugar as desired.

Enjoy these classic sugar cookies as-is or get creative with your decorations to make them festive for any holiday or occasion!

Gingerbread Cookies

Ingredients:

- 3 cups all-purpose flour
- 1 teaspoon baking soda
- 2 teaspoons ground ginger
- 1 1/2 teaspoons ground cinnamon
- 1/2 teaspoon ground cloves
- 1/2 teaspoon salt
- 1/2 cup unsalted butter, softened
- 1/2 cup packed brown sugar
- 1 large egg
- 1/2 cup molasses
- 1 teaspoon vanilla extract

Instructions:

1. Preheat Oven: Preheat your oven to 350°F (175°C) and line baking sheets with parchment paper.
2. Mix Dry Ingredients: In a medium bowl, whisk together the flour, baking soda, ginger, cinnamon, cloves, and salt. Set aside.
3. Cream Butter and Sugar: In a large mixing bowl, beat the softened butter and brown sugar together until light and fluffy.
4. Add Egg, Molasses, and Vanilla: Beat in the egg, molasses, and vanilla extract until well combined.
5. Incorporate Dry Ingredients: Gradually add the flour mixture to the wet ingredients, mixing until the dough comes together. The dough should be firm but not sticky. If it's too dry, add a tablespoon of water.
6. Chill Dough: Divide the dough into two equal portions, flatten into disks, wrap in plastic wrap, and refrigerate for at least 1 hour or until firm.
7. Roll and Cut: On a lightly floured surface, roll out one portion of the dough to about 1/4-inch thickness. Use cookie cutters to cut out desired shapes. Transfer the cut-out cookies to the prepared baking sheets, spacing them about 1 inch apart.
8. Bake: Bake in the preheated oven for 8-10 minutes or until the edges are set and just beginning to brown. Remove from the oven and let the cookies cool on the

baking sheets for a few minutes before transferring to a wire rack to cool completely.
9. Decorate (Optional): Once cooled, decorate the gingerbread cookies with icing, candies, or sprinkles. Have fun and get creative with your designs!

These gingerbread cookies can be enjoyed on their own or used to create festive decorations for the holidays. They also make wonderful edible gifts when packaged in decorative bags or boxes. Enjoy the warm, spicy flavors of homemade gingerbread!

Peppermint Bark

Ingredients:

- 12 ounces semi-sweet or dark chocolate, chopped (or use chocolate chips)
- 12 ounces white chocolate, chopped (or use white chocolate chips)
- 1 teaspoon peppermint extract
- 1/2 cup crushed candy canes or peppermint candies

Instructions:

1. Prepare Baking Sheet: Line a baking sheet with parchment paper or a silicone baking mat.
2. Melt Semi-Sweet/Dark Chocolate: Place the chopped semi-sweet or dark chocolate in a microwave-safe bowl. Microwave in 30-second intervals, stirring after each interval, until the chocolate is melted and smooth. Alternatively, you can melt the chocolate using a double boiler.
3. Spread Dark Chocolate: Pour the melted dark chocolate onto the prepared baking sheet. Use an offset spatula or the back of a spoon to spread it into an even layer, about 1/4-inch thick. Tap the baking sheet gently on the counter to smooth out the chocolate.
4. Chill Dark Chocolate: Place the baking sheet in the refrigerator for about 15-20 minutes or until the dark chocolate is set.
5. Melt White Chocolate: While the dark chocolate is chilling, melt the white chocolate using the same method as before (microwave or double boiler). Stir in the peppermint extract to the melted white chocolate.
6. Spread White Chocolate: Remove the baking sheet from the refrigerator. Pour the melted white chocolate over the chilled dark chocolate layer. Quickly spread it into an even layer using an offset spatula.
7. Sprinkle Crushed Peppermint: Immediately sprinkle the crushed candy canes or peppermint candies evenly over the melted white chocolate layer. Gently press the peppermint pieces into the chocolate.
8. Chill to Set: Return the baking sheet to the refrigerator and chill for another 30 minutes or until the peppermint bark is completely set and firm.
9. Break into Pieces: Once set, remove the peppermint bark from the refrigerator. Peel off the parchment paper and break the bark into pieces using your hands or a knife.

10. Enjoy: Serve the peppermint bark at room temperature and enjoy the delicious combination of chocolate and peppermint!

Store any leftover peppermint bark in an airtight container in the refrigerator for up to 2 weeks. It also makes a wonderful holiday gift when packaged in festive bags or boxes. Happy baking!

Pecan Pie Bars

Ingredients:

For the Crust:

- 1 1/2 cups all-purpose flour
- 1/2 cup granulated sugar
- 1/2 teaspoon salt
- 3/4 cup unsalted butter, cold and cut into small cubes

For the Pecan Filling:

- 3/4 cup unsalted butter
- 1 cup packed light brown sugar
- 1/2 cup honey or corn syrup
- 2 tablespoons heavy cream
- 4 cups pecan halves or chopped pecans
- 1 teaspoon vanilla extract
- 1/4 teaspoon salt

Instructions:

1. Preheat Oven: Preheat your oven to 350°F (175°C) and grease or line a 9x13-inch baking dish with parchment paper.
2. Make the Crust: In a mixing bowl, whisk together the flour, sugar, and salt. Add the cold cubed butter and use a pastry cutter or fork to cut the butter into the dry ingredients until the mixture resembles coarse crumbs. Press the mixture evenly into the bottom of the prepared baking dish.
3. Bake the Crust: Bake the crust in the preheated oven for 15-18 minutes or until lightly golden. Remove from the oven and set aside.
4. Prepare the Pecan Filling: In a medium saucepan, combine the butter, brown sugar, honey or corn syrup, and heavy cream. Cook over medium heat, stirring constantly, until the mixture comes to a boil.
5. Cook the Filling: Once boiling, continue to cook for 1 minute, then remove the saucepan from the heat. Stir in the pecans, vanilla extract, and salt until well combined.

6. Assemble and Bake: Pour the pecan filling evenly over the baked crust, spreading it out with a spatula. Return the baking dish to the oven and bake for an additional 20-25 minutes or until the filling is bubbling and set.
7. Cool and Slice: Remove the pecan pie bars from the oven and let them cool completely in the baking dish on a wire rack. Once cooled, lift the bars out of the dish using the parchment paper and transfer them to a cutting board. Cut into squares or bars using a sharp knife.
8. Serve: Serve the pecan pie bars at room temperature. They can be stored in an airtight container at room temperature for a few days or in the refrigerator for longer storage.

These pecan pie bars are perfect for holiday gatherings or as a sweet treat throughout the season. They offer all the deliciousness of pecan pie in a convenient handheld form! Enjoy baking and sharing these delightful bars with friends and family.

Chocolate Fudge

Ingredients:

- 3 cups semi-sweet chocolate chips
- 1 (14-ounce) can sweetened condensed milk
- 1/4 cup unsalted butter
- 1 teaspoon vanilla extract
- Optional: chopped nuts, marshmallows, or other mix-ins

Instructions:

1. Prepare Pan: Line an 8x8-inch square baking pan with parchment paper or aluminum foil, leaving some overhang for easy removal later. Lightly grease the lined pan with butter or cooking spray.
2. Melt Chocolate: In a medium saucepan, combine the chocolate chips, sweetened condensed milk, and butter over low heat. Stir continuously until the chocolate chips and butter have melted and the mixture is smooth and well combined. Be careful not to let it scorch.
3. Add Vanilla: Remove the saucepan from heat and stir in the vanilla extract until fully incorporated.
4. Optional Mix-ins: If desired, stir in chopped nuts, marshmallows, or any other mix-Ins of your choice at this point.
5. Pour into Pan: Pour the chocolate mixture into the prepared baking pan, spreading it out evenly with a spatula.
6. Chill to Set: Refrigerate the fudge for at least 2 hours or until completely set.
7. Cut into Pieces: Once the fudge is firm and set, lift it out of the pan using the overhang of parchment paper or foil. Place it on a cutting board and peel away the paper or foil. Use a sharp knife to cut the fudge into squares or rectangles.
8. Serve: Arrange the chocolate fudge pieces on a serving plate and enjoy! Store any leftovers in an airtight container in the refrigerator for up to two weeks.

You can also customize this chocolate fudge recipe by adding different flavors such as peppermint extract, orange zest, or a sprinkle of sea salt on top. It's a delightful homemade treat that makes a wonderful gift or addition to holiday dessert platters. Enjoy the rich and creamy goodness of homemade chocolate fudge!

Linzer Cookies

Ingredients:

- 1 cup unsalted butter, softened
- 2/3 cup granulated sugar
- 1 teaspoon vanilla extract
- 1 teaspoon almond extract
- 1 large egg
- 2 cups all-purpose flour
- 1 1/2 cups almond flour or finely ground almonds
- 1/2 teaspoon ground cinnamon
- 1/2 teaspoon salt
- 1/2 cup raspberry, strawberry, or apricot jam
- Powdered sugar, for dusting

Instructions:

1. Preheat Oven: Preheat your oven to 350°F (175°C) and line baking sheets with parchment paper.
2. Cream Butter and Sugar: In a large mixing bowl, cream together the softened butter and granulated sugar until light and fluffy.
3. Add Extracts and Egg: Beat in the vanilla extract, almond extract, and egg until well combined.
4. Mix Dry Ingredients: In a separate bowl, whisk together the all-purpose flour, almond flour (or ground almonds), cinnamon, and salt.
5. Combine Wet and Dry Mixtures: Gradually add the dry ingredients to the wet ingredients, mixing until a dough forms. If the dough is too sticky, you can refrigerate it for about 30 minutes to make it easier to handle.
6. Roll Out Dough: On a lightly floured surface, roll out the dough to about 1/4-inch thickness. Use a round cookie cutter (about 2 inches in diameter) to cut out cookies. Use a smaller cutter (such as a heart or star shape) to cut out the centers of half of the cookies. These will be the top halves of your Linzer cookies.
7. Bake: Place the cookies on the prepared baking sheets and bake in the preheated oven for 10-12 minutes or until the edges are lightly golden. Remove from the oven and let them cool on the baking sheets for a few minutes before transferring to a wire rack to cool completely.

8. Assemble the Cookies: Spread a thin layer of jam on the bottom halves (cookies without the cutout centers) of the cookies. Place the top halves (cookies with the cutout centers) on top of the jam-covered cookies.
9. Dust with Powdered Sugar: Right before serving, dust the tops of the Linzer cookies with powdered sugar using a fine mesh sieve.
10. Enjoy: Serve and enjoy these delightful Linzer cookies with a cup of tea or coffee!

These cookies are not only delicious but also beautifully festive with their jam-filled centers and decorative powdered sugar topping. They make a lovely addition to holiday cookie platters and are sure to be a hit with family and friends.

Rum Balls

Ingredients:

- 2 cups vanilla wafer cookies, finely crushed
- 1 cup powdered sugar
- 1 cup finely chopped pecans or walnuts
- 2 tablespoons unsweetened cocoa powder
- 1/4 cup dark rum (or to taste)
- 2 tablespoons honey or corn syrup
- Additional powdered sugar or cocoa powder, for coating

Instructions:

1. Prepare Ingredients: In a large bowl, combine the finely crushed vanilla wafer cookies, powdered sugar, chopped nuts, and cocoa powder.
2. Add Rum and Sweetener: Pour in the dark rum and honey or corn syrup. Mix well until the mixture comes together and can be easily shaped into balls. The mixture should be moist but not too wet.
3. Shape into Balls: Using your hands, scoop out portions of the mixture and roll them into small balls, about 1 inch in diameter. Place the balls on a baking sheet lined with parchment paper.
4. Coat with Powdered Sugar or Cocoa: Roll each rum ball in powdered sugar or cocoa powder to coat evenly. You can also use a combination of both for a decorative finish.
5. Chill to Set: Refrigerate the rum balls for at least 1 hour or until firm. This helps them set and develop their flavors.
6. Serve and Enjoy: Once chilled, transfer the rum balls to an airtight container and store them in the refrigerator until ready to serve. They can be enjoyed immediately or kept for several days.

Rum balls make a delightful addition to holiday dessert platters or can be wrapped up as homemade gifts for friends and family. They have a rich, chocolatey flavor with a hint of rum that's sure to please anyone with a sweet tooth. Enjoy these boozy treats responsibly and savor their deliciousness during the festive season!

Eggnog Cheesecake

Ingredients:

For the Crust:

- 1 1/2 cups graham cracker crumbs
- 1/4 cup granulated sugar
- 1/2 cup unsalted butter, melted

For the Cheesecake Filling:

- 24 ounces (3 packages) cream cheese, softened
- 1 cup granulated sugar
- 3 large eggs
- 1 cup eggnog
- 1/4 cup all-purpose flour
- 1 tablespoon rum or bourbon (optional)
- 1 teaspoon vanilla extract
- 1/2 teaspoon ground nutmeg
- Pinch of salt

For the Topping (optional):

- Whipped cream
- Ground nutmeg
- Cinnamon sticks (for garnish)

Instructions:

1. Preheat Oven and Prepare Pan: Preheat your oven to 325°F (160°C). Grease a 9-inch springform pan with butter and line the bottom with parchment paper.
2. Make the Crust: In a medium bowl, combine the graham cracker crumbs, sugar, and melted butter. Mix until the crumbs are moistened. Press the mixture evenly into the bottom of the prepared springform pan. Use the back of a spoon or a flat-bottomed glass to pack the crust firmly. Set aside.
3. Prepare the Cheesecake Filling: In a large mixing bowl, beat the softened cream cheese and sugar together until smooth and creamy, about 2-3 minutes.
4. Add Eggs and Eggnog: Add the eggs, one at a time, beating well after each addition. Gradually add the eggnog, flour, rum or bourbon (if using), vanilla

extract, ground nutmeg, and salt. Mix until all ingredients are well combined and the batter is smooth.
5. Pour and Bake: Pour the cheesecake filling over the prepared crust in the springform pan. Smooth the top with a spatula.
6. Bake in Water Bath (Optional): To prevent cracking, you can place the springform pan inside a larger baking pan and fill the larger pan with hot water halfway up the sides of the springform pan.
7. Bake the Cheesecake: Bake in the preheated oven for 60-70 minutes or until the edges are set and the center is slightly jiggly. The cheesecake will continue to set as it cools.
8. Cool and Chill: Remove the cheesecake from the oven and let it cool in the pan on a wire rack for 10 minutes. Then run a knife around the edges of the cheesecake to loosen it from the pan. Allow it to cool completely, then cover and refrigerate for at least 4 hours or overnight.
9. Serve: When ready to serve, carefully remove the sides of the springform pan. If desired, garnish the top of the cheesecake with whipped cream, a sprinkle of ground nutmeg, and cinnamon sticks.
10. Enjoy: Slice and serve chilled. Enjoy the creamy and festive flavors of eggnog cheesecake!

This eggnog cheesecake is perfect for holiday gatherings and celebrations. It's rich, creamy, and has just the right amount of eggnog flavor to evoke the spirit of the season. Happy baking!

Stollen (German Christmas bread)

Ingredients:

For the Stollen:

- 1 cup mixed dried fruit (such as raisins, currants, candied citrus peel)
- 1/2 cup chopped dried apricots
- 1/4 cup rum or orange juice
- 1/2 cup warm milk
- 2 1/4 teaspoons (1 packet) active dry yeast
- 1/4 cup granulated sugar
- 3 1/2 cups all-purpose flour
- 1/2 teaspoon salt
- 1/2 teaspoon ground nutmeg
- 1/2 teaspoon ground cinnamon
- Zest of 1 lemon
- Zest of 1 orange
- 1/2 cup unsalted butter, softened
- 2 large eggs
- 1 cup slivered almonds
- 1/2 cup candied cherries (optional)

For Finishing:

- 1/2 cup unsalted butter, melted
- Powdered sugar, for dusting

Instructions:

1. Prepare the Dried Fruit: In a bowl, combine the mixed dried fruit and chopped dried apricots with rum or orange juice. Let it soak for at least 1 hour or overnight, until the fruits plump up.
2. Activate the Yeast: In a small bowl, combine warm milk and yeast. Stir in a pinch of sugar and let it sit for 5-10 minutes until foamy.
3. Mix the Dough: In a large mixing bowl or stand mixer fitted with a dough hook, combine the flour, sugar, salt, nutmeg, cinnamon, lemon zest, and orange zest. Add the softened butter, eggs, and yeast mixture. Mix until the dough starts to come together.

4. **Knead the Dough:** Turn the dough out onto a lightly floured surface and knead for about 8-10 minutes, until smooth and elastic. Alternatively, continue kneading with the stand mixer for the same amount of time.
5. **Incorporate Fruits and Nuts:** Drain the soaked dried fruit mixture and add it to the dough along with slivered almonds and candied cherries (if using). Knead gently until the fruits and nuts are evenly distributed throughout the dough.
6. **First Rise:** Place the dough in a greased bowl, cover with a clean kitchen towel, and let it rise in a warm place for 1-2 hours, or until doubled in size.
7. **Shape the Stollen:** Punch down the risen dough and divide it in half. Roll each half into an oval shape, then fold one side over the other to form a loaf shape. Place the loaves on a parchment-lined baking sheet.
8. **Second Rise:** Cover the loaves loosely with a kitchen towel and let them rise again for 30-45 minutes.
9. **Preheat Oven:** Preheat your oven to 350°F (175°C) while the loaves are rising.
10. **Bake the Stollen:** Bake the Stollen loaves in the preheated oven for 25-30 minutes, or until golden brown and cooked through.
11. **Finishing:** Remove the Stollen from the oven and immediately brush them with melted butter. Let them cool on a wire rack.
12. **Dust with Powdered Sugar:** Once cooled, generously dust the Stollen with powdered sugar.
13. **Serve and Enjoy:** Slice and serve the Stollen as is, or with butter and a cup of hot tea or mulled wine.

Stollen can be made ahead of time and stored wrapped in foil or plastic wrap at room temperature for several days, allowing the flavors to develop. It also makes a wonderful holiday gift when packaged beautifully. Enjoy the festive flavors of homemade Stollen!

Yule Log Cake (Bûche de Noël)

Ingredients:

For the Cake:

- 4 large eggs, separated
- 3/4 cup granulated sugar, divided
- 1 teaspoon vanilla extract
- 1/4 cup all-purpose flour
- 1/4 cup cocoa powder
- 1/4 teaspoon salt

For the Filling:

- 1 1/2 cups heavy cream
- 3 tablespoons powdered sugar
- 1 teaspoon vanilla extract

For the Chocolate Buttercream Frosting:

- 1/2 cup unsalted butter, softened
- 1 cup powdered sugar
- 1/4 cup cocoa powder
- 1/2 teaspoon vanilla extract
- 1-2 tablespoons heavy cream (if needed)

For Decoration (optional):

- Powdered sugar (for dusting)
- Meringue mushrooms
- Fresh berries
- Sprigs of rosemary or other greenery

Instructions:

1. Preheat Oven: Preheat your oven to 375°F (190°C). Grease a 10x15-inch jelly roll pan (or rimmed baking sheet) and line it with parchment paper.
2. Make the Cake: In a large mixing bowl, beat the egg yolks with 1/2 cup of granulated sugar until pale and thick. Stir in the vanilla extract.

3. **Sift Dry Ingredients:** In a separate bowl, sift together the flour, cocoa powder, and salt.
4. **Fold in Dry Ingredients:** Gradually fold the dry ingredients into the egg yolk mixture until just combined.
5. **Whip Egg Whites:** In another clean bowl, beat the egg whites until soft peaks form. Gradually add the remaining 1/4 cup of granulated sugar and continue beating until stiff peaks form.
6. **Combine Batter:** Gently fold the whipped egg whites into the egg yolk mixture until no streaks remain.
7. **Bake:** Spread the batter evenly into the prepared jelly roll pan. Bake in the preheated oven for 12-15 minutes, or until the cake springs back when lightly touched.
8. **Prepare Filling:** While the cake is baking, make the filling. In a mixing bowl, whip the heavy cream, powdered sugar, and vanilla extract until stiff peaks form. Refrigerate until ready to use.
9. **Roll the Cake:** Dust a clean kitchen towel with powdered sugar. Immediately invert the baked cake onto the towel and carefully peel off the parchment paper. Roll the cake tightly with the towel from the short end and let it cool completely.
10. **Make Buttercream Frosting:** In a mixing bowl, beat the softened butter until creamy. Gradually add the powdered sugar, cocoa powder, and vanilla extract, beating until smooth and fluffy. Add heavy cream if needed to reach a spreadable consistency.
11. **Assemble the Bûche de Noël:** Carefully unroll the cooled cake from the towel. Spread the prepared whipped cream filling evenly over the cake, leaving a small border around the edges. Roll the cake back up without the towel, starting from the same short end.
12. **Frost the Cake:** Trim the ends of the rolled cake at an angle and place the cake seam side down on a serving platter. Frost the entire cake with the chocolate buttercream, using a fork to create a bark-like texture.
13. **Decorate:** Use a knife to create a bark-like pattern on the frosting. Dust with powdered sugar for a snowy effect. Decorate with meringue mushrooms, fresh berries, and greenery to resemble a woodland log.
14. **Chill and Serve:** Refrigerate the Bûche de Noël for at least 1 hour before serving to set the frosting and filling. Slice and enjoy this festive and delightful holiday dessert!

The Bûche de Noël is a stunning and delicious centerpiece for any holiday gathering. It's a delightful treat that captures the spirit of the season with its festive decorations and flavors. Enjoy making and sharing this special cake with loved ones!

Rugelach

Ingredients:

For the Dough:

- 1 cup unsalted butter, softened
- 8 ounces cream cheese, softened
- 1/4 cup granulated sugar
- 1 teaspoon vanilla extract
- 2 cups all-purpose flour
- 1/4 teaspoon salt

For the Filling:

- 1/2 cup fruit preserves (such as raspberry or apricot)
- 1/2 cup finely chopped nuts (such as walnuts or pecans)
- 1/2 cup packed brown sugar
- 1 teaspoon ground cinnamon
- 1/2 cup mini chocolate chips (optional)
- Additional granulated sugar, for sprinkling

Instructions:

1. Make the Dough: In a large mixing bowl or stand mixer, cream together the softened butter, cream cheese, and granulated sugar until smooth and fluffy. Add the vanilla extract and mix until combined.
2. Add Flour and Salt: Gradually add the flour and salt to the creamed mixture, mixing until a dough forms. Divide the dough into four equal portions, shape each into a disk, wrap in plastic wrap, and refrigerate for at least 1 hour (or up to overnight).
3. Prepare the Filling: In a small bowl, combine the fruit preserves, chopped nuts, brown sugar, cinnamon, and mini chocolate chips (if using). Mix until well combined. Set aside.
4. Assemble the Rugelach:
    - Preheat your oven to 350°F (175°C) and line baking sheets with parchment paper.

- Take one dough disk out of the refrigerator and roll it out on a lightly floured surface into a 10-inch circle.
- Spread about 2-3 tablespoons of the filling evenly over the dough circle, leaving a small border around the edges.
- Use a pizza cutter or sharp knife to cut the circle into 12 equal wedges.
- Starting from the wide end, roll up each wedge to form a crescent shape.
- Place the rugelach on the prepared baking sheets, seam side down.
- Repeat the process with the remaining dough disks and filling.

5. Bake the Rugelach: Lightly brush the rugelach with water or beaten egg and sprinkle with granulated sugar.
   - Bake in the preheated oven for 20-25 minutes, or until golden brown and flaky.
   - Remove from the oven and let cool on the baking sheets for a few minutes, then transfer to wire racks to cool completely.
6. Serve and Enjoy: Rugelach can be served at room temperature. Store any leftovers in an airtight container at room temperature for several days, or freeze for longer storage.

Rugelach is a delightful pastry that can be enjoyed as a sweet treat with coffee or tea.

It's perfect for holiday gatherings, brunches, or simply as a homemade snack.

Customize the fillings according to your preferences for a personalized touch. Enjoy baking and savoring these delicious rugelach!

Panettone

Ingredients:

For the Sponge:

- 1/2 cup bread flour
- 1/4 cup warm water
- 1 packet (2 1/4 teaspoons) active dry yeast
- 1 tablespoon granulated sugar

For the Dough:

- 3 large eggs, at room temperature
- 1/3 cup granulated sugar
- 1 tablespoon honey
- Zest of 1 orange
- Zest of 1 lemon
- 1 teaspoon vanilla extract
- 3/4 cup unsalted butter, softened
- 2 cups bread flour, plus more as needed
- 1/2 teaspoon salt
- 1/2 cup golden raisins
- 1/2 cup mixed candied citrus peel
- Additional butter, for greasing
- Powdered sugar, for dusting (optional)

Instructions:

1. Make the Sponge: In a small bowl, combine 1/2 cup bread flour, warm water, yeast, and 1 tablespoon sugar. Mix well to form a thick batter. Cover the bowl with plastic wrap and let it rest in a warm place for about 1 hour, or until bubbly and doubled in size.
2. Prepare the Dough: In a large mixing bowl or stand mixer bowl, beat together the eggs, sugar, honey, orange zest, lemon zest, and vanilla extract until well combined.
3. Add Sponge and Butter: Stir in the sponge mixture, then gradually add the softened butter, mixing until incorporated.

4. Incorporate Flour and Salt: Gradually add 2 cups of bread flour and salt to the wet ingredients, mixing until a soft dough forms. If the dough is too sticky, add more flour, a tablespoon at a time, until the dough pulls away from the sides of the bowl.
5. Knead the Dough: Turn the dough out onto a lightly floured surface and knead for about 10-15 minutes, or until smooth and elastic. Alternatively, knead the dough using a stand mixer fitted with a dough hook.
6. Add Dried Fruits: Knead in the golden raisins and candied citrus peel until evenly distributed throughout the dough.
7. First Rise: Place the dough in a greased bowl, cover with plastic wrap, and let it rise in a warm place for 2-3 hours, or until doubled in size.
8. Shape the Panettone: Punch down the risen dough and transfer it to a panettone mold or large, greased and floured deep cake pan. Alternatively, you can use a large, parchment-lined coffee can or similar container. Shape the dough into a round, domed loaf.
9. Second Rise: Cover the shaped dough loosely with plastic wrap and let it rise in a warm place for another 2-3 hours, or until puffed up and nearly doubled in size.
10. Bake: Preheat your oven to 350°F (175°C). Bake the panettone for 40-50 minutes, or until golden brown and a skewer inserted into the center comes out clean. If the top begins to brown too quickly, cover it loosely with aluminum foil.
11. Cool and Serve: Remove the panettone from the oven and let it cool in the mold or pan for about 10 minutes before transferring to a wire rack to cool completely. Dust with powdered sugar before serving, if desired.
12. Enjoy: Slice and enjoy your homemade panettone with a cup of coffee or tea. It's perfect for sharing with family and friends during the holiday season!

Homemade panettone is a labor of love, but the taste and texture are truly exceptional. This recipe will yield a delicious, festive bread that captures the essence of traditional Italian baking. Enjoy the process and savor the flavors of this classic holiday treat!

Cranberry Orange Scones

Ingredients:

- 2 cups all-purpose flour
- 1/3 cup granulated sugar
- 1 tablespoon baking powder
- 1/2 teaspoon salt
- Zest of 1 large orange
- 1/2 cup cold unsalted butter, cut into small pieces
- 1/2 cup dried cranberries (or fresh/frozen cranberries, chopped)
- 1/2 cup heavy cream
- 1/4 cup fresh orange juice
- 1 teaspoon vanilla extract
- Optional: coarse sugar for sprinkling on top

For the Glaze (Optional):

- 1 cup powdered sugar
- 2-3 tablespoons fresh orange juice
- Zest of 1 orange (optional)

Instructions:

1. Preheat Oven: Preheat your oven to 400°F (200°C). Line a baking sheet with parchment paper or silicone mat.
2. Mix Dry Ingredients: In a large bowl, whisk together the flour, sugar, baking powder, salt, and orange zest.
3. Cut in Butter: Add the cold butter pieces to the flour mixture. Using a pastry cutter or your fingers, cut the butter into the flour until the mixture resembles coarse crumbs with pea-sized butter pieces.
4. Add Cranberries: Gently stir in the dried cranberries until evenly distributed in the flour mixture.
5. Combine Wet Ingredients: In a separate bowl, whisk together the heavy cream, orange juice, and vanilla extract.
6. Form Dough: Make a well in the center of the dry ingredients and pour in the wet ingredients. Stir with a fork or spatula until the dough begins to come together. Be careful not to overmix.

7. Shape and Cut Scones: Turn the dough out onto a lightly floured surface. Pat or gently roll the dough into a circle about 1 inch thick. Use a knife or bench scraper to cut the dough into 8 wedges.
8. Bake: Transfer the scones to the prepared baking sheet, leaving space between each scone. Optionally, brush the tops of the scones with a little heavy cream and sprinkle with coarse sugar.
9. Bake: Bake in the preheated oven for 15-18 minutes, or until the scones are golden brown on top and cooked through.
10. Make Glaze (Optional): While the scones are cooling, whisk together the powdered sugar, orange juice, and orange zest (if using) to make the glaze. Adjust the consistency by adding more or less orange juice as needed.
11. Glaze and Serve: Drizzle the glaze over the cooled scones. Allow the glaze to set for a few minutes before serving.
12. Enjoy: Serve these delightful Cranberry Orange Scones warm or at room temperature with a cup of tea or coffee.

These Cranberry Orange Scones are perfect for holiday breakfasts or brunches. They are best enjoyed fresh but can be stored in an airtight container at room temperature for a day or two. Simply reheat in the microwave for a few seconds if desired. Enjoy these tender, flavorful scones with bursts of cranberry and citrus goodness!

Snowball Cookies (Russian Tea Cakes)

Ingredients:

- 1 cup unsalted butter, softened
- 1/2 cup powdered sugar, plus more for coating
- 1 teaspoon vanilla extract
- 2 1/4 cups all-purpose flour
- 1/4 teaspoon salt
- 1 cup finely chopped pecans, walnuts, or almonds

Instructions:

1. Preheat Oven: Preheat your oven to 350°F (175°C). Line a baking sheet with parchment paper or silicone baking mat.
2. Cream Butter and Sugar: In a large mixing bowl, cream together the softened butter and 1/2 cup powdered sugar until light and fluffy.
3. Add Vanilla: Mix in the vanilla extract until well combined.
4. Add Flour and Salt: Gradually add the flour and salt to the butter mixture, mixing until a dough forms.
5. Incorporate Chopped Nuts: Fold in the finely chopped nuts until evenly distributed throughout the dough.
6. Shape into Balls: Take small portions of the dough (about 1 tablespoon each) and roll them into balls using your hands. Place the balls on the prepared baking sheet, spacing them about 1 inch apart.
7. Bake: Bake the cookies in the preheated oven for 12-15 minutes, or until set but not browned.
8. Cool: Allow the cookies to cool slightly on the baking sheet for a few minutes.
9. Coat in Powdered Sugar: While the cookies are still warm, gently roll them in powdered sugar until fully coated. Place the powdered sugar-coated cookies on a wire rack to cool completely.
10. Re-coat with Powdered Sugar: Once the cookies have cooled, roll them in powdered sugar again to ensure a thick, snowy coating.
11. Serve and Enjoy: Arrange the Snowball Cookies on a serving platter and enjoy these delightful treats with a cup of tea or coffee.

Snowball Cookies can be stored in an airtight container at room temperature for several days. The powdered sugar coating may absorb into the cookies over time, so you can give them another light dusting of powdered sugar before serving if desired. These cookies are perfect for holiday cookie exchanges and make lovely homemade gifts. Enjoy the buttery, nutty goodness of Snowball Cookies!

Holiday Fruitcake

Ingredients:

- 2 cups mixed candied fruits (such as cherries, pineapple, citron)
- 1 cup dried fruits (such as raisins, currants, chopped dates)
- 1 cup chopped nuts (such as pecans, walnuts)
- 1/2 cup dark rum or brandy (for soaking)
- 2 1/4 cups all-purpose flour
- 1 teaspoon baking powder
- 1/2 teaspoon salt
- 1 cup unsalted butter, softened
- 1 cup granulated sugar
- 4 large eggs
- 1/4 cup orange juice
- Zest of 1 orange
- Zest of 1 lemon
- 1 teaspoon vanilla extract
- 1/2 teaspoon almond extract

Instructions:

1. Prepare the Fruits and Nuts: In a large bowl, combine the mixed candied fruits, dried fruits, and chopped nuts. Pour the dark rum or brandy over the fruits and nuts, toss to combine, and let them soak overnight or for at least 4 hours.
2. Preheat Oven: Preheat your oven to 300°F (150°C). Grease and flour a 9x5-inch loaf pan or a round cake pan, or line with parchment paper.
3. Prepare Dry Ingredients: In a separate bowl, whisk together the flour, baking powder, and salt. Set aside.
4. Cream Butter and Sugar: In a large mixing bowl, cream together the softened butter and granulated sugar until light and fluffy.
5. Add Eggs and Flavorings: Beat in the eggs, one at a time, mixing well after each addition. Stir in the orange juice, orange zest, lemon zest, vanilla extract, and almond extract.
6. Combine Wet and Dry Ingredients: Gradually add the flour mixture to the wet ingredients, mixing until just combined.
7. Fold in Fruits and Nuts: Gently fold in the soaked fruits and nuts until evenly distributed throughout the batter.

8. Bake the Fruitcake: Pour the batter into the prepared loaf pan or cake pan, spreading it evenly. Smooth the top with a spatula.
9. Bake in Oven: Bake in the preheated oven for 2 to 2 1/2 hours, or until a toothpick inserted into the center of the cake comes out clean. If the top of the cake is browning too quickly, cover loosely with aluminum foil during baking.
10. Cool and Serve: Remove the fruitcake from the oven and let it cool in the pan for about 10 minutes. Then transfer the cake to a wire rack to cool completely.
11. Aging (Optional): For best flavor, wrap the cooled fruitcake in plastic wrap or aluminum foil and let it age for a few days to a few weeks. This allows the flavors to meld and develop.
12. Serve: Slice and serve the holiday fruitcake at room temperature. It's delicious enjoyed on its own or with a cup of tea or coffee.
13. Storage: Store any leftover fruitcake in an airtight container at room temperature for up to several weeks. You can also wrap it well and freeze for longer storage.

Holiday fruitcake is a festive and nostalgic dessert that is perfect for celebrating special occasions with family and friends. Enjoy the rich flavors and textures of this classic treat!

Candy Cane Macarons

Ingredients:

For the Macaron Shells:

- 1 cup confectioners' sugar
- 3/4 cup almond flour
- 2 large egg whites, at room temperature
- 1/4 cup granulated sugar
- Red gel food coloring (optional)

For the Peppermint Chocolate Ganache Filling:

- 4 ounces semi-sweet chocolate, finely chopped
- 1/2 cup heavy cream
- 1/2 teaspoon peppermint extract
- Crushed candy canes, for garnish

Instructions:

1. Prepare Macaron Shells:

- Line two baking sheets with parchment paper or silicone mats.
- In a food processor, combine confectioners' sugar and almond flour. Pulse until fine and well combined.
- Sift the almond flour mixture into a large bowl. Discard any larger bits that remain in the sieve.
- In a separate bowl, beat the egg whites with an electric mixer until foamy. Gradually add granulated sugar while continuing to beat. Beat until stiff peaks form and the meringue is glossy.
- Add a few drops of red gel food coloring to the meringue, if desired, and gently fold to incorporate.
- Add half of the sifted almond flour mixture to the meringue. Gently fold until just combined. Add the remaining almond flour mixture and continue folding until the batter is smooth and flows like lava.

- Transfer the batter to a piping bag fitted with a round tip. Pipe small circles (about 1 inch in diameter) onto the prepared baking sheets, spacing them about 1 inch apart.
- Tap the baking sheets on the counter a few times to release air bubbles. Let the piped macarons sit at room temperature for 30-60 minutes, until a skin forms on top and they are no longer sticky to the touch.

2. Bake and Cool:

- Preheat your oven to 300°F (150°C).
- Bake the macarons, one baking sheet at a time, for 15-18 minutes, rotating the pan halfway through baking.
- Remove from the oven and let the macarons cool completely on the baking sheets before removing them.

3. Prepare Peppermint Chocolate Ganache Filling:

- Place the chopped chocolate in a heatproof bowl.
- In a small saucepan, heat the heavy cream over medium heat until it just begins to simmer.
- Pour the hot cream over the chopped chocolate. Let it sit for 1-2 minutes, then stir until smooth and creamy.
- Stir in the peppermint extract. Let the ganache cool and thicken slightly.

4. Assemble the Macarons:

- Pair up the cooled macaron shells by size.
- Spoon or pipe a small amount of the peppermint chocolate ganache onto the flat side of one macaron shell.
- Top with another shell to form a sandwich. Press gently to spread the filling to the edges.
- Roll the edges of the filled macarons in crushed candy canes for decoration.
- Repeat with the remaining macaron shells and filling.

5. Chill and Serve:

- Place the filled macarons in an airtight container and refrigerate for at least 24 hours to mature.
- Bring the macarons to room temperature before serving.
- Enjoy these festive Candy Cane Macarons as a delightful holiday treat!

These Candy Cane Macarons are sure to impress with their delicate texture and festive flavors. They make a lovely addition to any holiday dessert spread or gift box. Enjoy making and sharing these delightful treats with loved ones!

Almond Biscotti

Ingredients:

- 2 cups all-purpose flour
- 1 cup granulated sugar
- 1 teaspoon baking powder
- 1/2 teaspoon salt
- 3 large eggs
- 1 teaspoon vanilla extract
- 1/2 teaspoon almond extract
- 1 cup whole almonds, toasted and roughly chopped

Optional Glaze:

- 1 cup powdered sugar
- 2-3 tablespoons milk or water
- 1/2 teaspoon almond extract

Instructions:

1. Preheat Oven: Preheat your oven to 350°F (175°C). Line a baking sheet with parchment paper.
2. Toast Almonds: Spread the almonds on a baking sheet and toast in the preheated oven for 8-10 minutes, or until lightly golden and fragrant. Let them cool, then roughly chop them.
3. Mix Dry Ingredients: In a large bowl, whisk together the flour, sugar, baking powder, and salt.
4. Combine Wet Ingredients: In another bowl, whisk together the eggs, vanilla extract, and almond extract.
5. Form Dough: Gradually add the egg mixture to the dry ingredients, stirring until a stiff dough forms. Fold in the toasted and chopped almonds.
6. Shape the Dough: Divide the dough in half. On a lightly floured surface, shape each half into a log about 12 inches long and 2 inches wide. Place the logs on the prepared baking sheet, spacing them apart.
7. Bake: Bake in the preheated oven for 25-30 minutes, or until the logs are firm to the touch and lightly golden.

8. Cool: Remove the baking sheet from the oven and let the logs cool on a wire rack for about 15 minutes. Reduce the oven temperature to 325°F (160°C).
9. Slice the Biscotti: Transfer the cooled logs to a cutting board. Using a sharp serrated knife, slice each log diagonally into 1/2-inch thick slices.
10. Second Bake: Arrange the biscotti slices cut-side down on the baking sheet. Bake for 10-12 minutes, then carefully flip the biscotti and bake for an additional 10-12 minutes, or until golden and crisp.
11. Optional Glaze: If desired, whisk together powdered sugar, milk or water, and almond extract to make a glaze. Drizzle the glaze over the cooled biscotti and let it set before serving.
12. Serve and Store: Let the almond biscotti cool completely on a wire rack before serving. Store in an airtight container at room temperature for up to two weeks.

Almond biscotti are perfect for enjoying as a snack or dessert. They also make lovely gifts when packaged beautifully. Serve them alongside your favorite hot beverage for a delightful treat!

Cinnamon Rolls

Ingredients:

For the Dough:

- 1 cup warm milk (about 110°F or 43°C)
- 2 1/4 teaspoons (1 packet) active dry yeast
- 1/2 cup granulated sugar
- 1/3 cup unsalted butter, melted
- 2 large eggs, room temperature
- 4 1/2 cups all-purpose flour
- 1 teaspoon salt

For the Filling:

- 1 cup packed brown sugar
- 2 1/2 tablespoons ground cinnamon
- 1/3 cup unsalted butter, softened

For the Cream Cheese Frosting:

- 4 ounces cream cheese, softened
- 1/4 cup unsalted butter, softened
- 1 cup powdered sugar
- 1/2 teaspoon vanilla extract

Instructions:

1. Activate Yeast: In a small bowl, combine warm milk, yeast, and 1 tablespoon of granulated sugar. Let it sit for about 5-10 minutes until frothy.
2. Prepare Dough: In a large mixing bowl or the bowl of a stand mixer fitted with a dough hook, combine the activated yeast mixture with the remaining sugar, melted butter, eggs, flour, and salt. Mix until the dough comes together.
3. Knead the Dough: Knead the dough by hand on a floured surface or with the stand mixer for about 5-7 minutes until smooth and elastic. Add more flour if the dough is too sticky.
4. First Rise: Place the dough in a greased bowl, cover with a clean kitchen towel, and let it rise in a warm place for about 1-1.5 hours until doubled in size.

5. Prepare Filling: In a small bowl, mix together brown sugar and cinnamon for the filling.
6. Roll Out Dough: Punch down the risen dough and transfer it to a floured surface. Roll out the dough into a rectangle about 16x20 inches.
7. Fill and Roll: Spread softened butter over the dough rectangle, leaving a small border around the edges. Sprinkle the cinnamon sugar mixture evenly over the butter.
8. Roll the Dough: Starting from one long edge, tightly roll up the dough into a log. Pinch the seam to seal.
9. Cut into Rolls: Using a sharp knife or unflavored dental floss, cut the log into 12 equal slices.
10. Second Rise: Place the cinnamon rolls in a greased 9x13-inch baking pan or two 9-inch round cake pans. Cover with a kitchen towel and let them rise for another 30-45 minutes until puffy.
11. Preheat Oven: Preheat your oven to 375°F (190°C).
12. Bake the Rolls: Bake the cinnamon rolls in the preheated oven for 20-25 minutes or until golden brown.
13. Make Cream Cheese Frosting: While the rolls are baking, prepare the cream cheese frosting. In a mixing bowl, beat together cream cheese, softened butter, powdered sugar, and vanilla extract until smooth and creamy.
14. Frost the Rolls: Spread the cream cheese frosting over the warm cinnamon rolls as soon as they come out of the oven.
15. Serve and Enjoy: Serve the cinnamon rolls warm and enjoy!

These homemade cinnamon rolls are best enjoyed fresh on the day they are made. They can also be stored in an airtight container at room temperature for a day or two. Microwave briefly before serving to reheat if desired. Enjoy the delicious aroma and taste of freshly baked cinnamon rolls!

Pumpkin Pie

Ingredients:

For the Pie Crust:

- 1 1/4 cups all-purpose flour
- 1/2 teaspoon salt
- 1/2 cup cold unsalted butter, cut into small cubes
- 3-4 tablespoons ice water

For the Pumpkin Filling:

- 1 (15-ounce) can pumpkin puree (or homemade pumpkin puree)
- 3/4 cup packed light brown sugar
- 2 large eggs
- 1 cup heavy cream (or evaporated milk)
- 1 teaspoon vanilla extract
- 1 teaspoon ground cinnamon
- 1/2 teaspoon ground ginger
- 1/4 teaspoon ground nutmeg
- 1/4 teaspoon ground cloves
- 1/2 teaspoon salt

Instructions:

1. Prepare the Pie Crust:

- In a large mixing bowl, whisk together the flour and salt.
- Add the cold cubed butter to the flour mixture. Use a pastry cutter or fork to cut the butter into the flour until the mixture resembles coarse crumbs.
- Gradually add ice water, 1 tablespoon at a time, mixing with a fork, until the dough begins to come together.
- Gather the dough into a ball, flatten into a disk, wrap in plastic wrap, and refrigerate for at least 1 hour.

2. Roll Out and Pre-Bake the Crust:

- Preheat your oven to 375°F (190°C).
- On a lightly floured surface, roll out the chilled dough into a 12-inch circle.
- Carefully transfer the dough to a 9-inch pie dish. Trim any excess dough and crimp the edges as desired.
- Line the crust with parchment paper or foil and fill with pie weights or dried beans.
- Bake in the preheated oven for 15 minutes. Remove the parchment paper and weights, then bake for an additional 5-7 minutes until the crust is set and lightly golden. Remove from the oven and let it cool slightly.

3. Make the Pumpkin Filling:

- In a large mixing bowl, whisk together the pumpkin puree, brown sugar, eggs, heavy cream, vanilla extract, spices (cinnamon, ginger, nutmeg, cloves), and salt until smooth and well combined.

4. Assemble and Bake the Pie:

- Pour the pumpkin filling into the pre-baked pie crust.
- Place the pie in the oven (still at 375°F) and bake for 45-50 minutes, or until the filling is set around the edges but slightly jiggly in the center.
- If the crust edges start to brown too quickly, cover them with a pie crust shield or foil strips.
- Remove the pie from the oven and let it cool completely on a wire rack.
- Refrigerate the cooled pie for at least 4 hours or overnight to set before serving.

5. Serve and Enjoy:

- Slice the chilled pumpkin pie and serve with whipped cream or vanilla ice cream, if desired.
- Enjoy this delicious homemade pumpkin pie as a delightful fall or holiday dessert!

This pumpkin pie is sure to be a hit at any gathering. The combination of warm spices and creamy pumpkin filling nestled in a flaky crust is simply irresistible. Happy baking!

Mince Pies

Ingredients:

For the Mincemeat Filling:

- 1 cup mixed dried fruits (such as raisins, currants, sultanas)
- 1/2 cup chopped apples (peeled and cored)
- 1/4 cup chopped almonds or walnuts
- Zest and juice of 1 orange
- Zest and juice of 1 lemon
- 1/2 cup dark brown sugar
- 1/4 cup unsalted butter, melted
- 1/2 teaspoon ground cinnamon
- 1/4 teaspoon ground nutmeg
- 1/4 teaspoon ground cloves
- 1/4 teaspoon ground ginger
- 1/4 cup brandy or rum (optional)

For the Pastry:

- 2 1/2 cups all-purpose flour
- 1/2 cup powdered sugar
- 1 cup cold unsalted butter, cut into cubes
- 1 large egg, beaten (for egg wash)
- Additional powdered sugar, for dusting

Instructions:

1. Make the Mincemeat Filling:

- In a large mixing bowl, combine the mixed dried fruits, chopped apples, chopped nuts, orange zest, lemon zest, orange juice, lemon juice, dark brown sugar, melted butter, and spices (cinnamon, nutmeg, cloves, ginger).
- If using, add brandy or rum to the mixture and stir well to combine.
- Cover the bowl and let the mincemeat filling macerate for at least 1 hour, or overnight in the refrigerator.

2. Prepare the Pastry:

- In a food processor, combine the flour and powdered sugar. Add the cold cubed butter and pulse until the mixture resembles coarse crumbs.
- Gradually add cold water, 1 tablespoon at a time, and pulse until the dough just begins to come together.
- Turn the dough out onto a lightly floured surface and knead briefly until smooth. Divide the dough into two portions, wrap each in plastic wrap, and refrigerate for at least 30 minutes.

3. Assemble the Mince Pies:

- Preheat your oven to 375°F (190°C). Grease a 12-cup muffin tin.
- Roll out one portion of the chilled pastry dough on a lightly floured surface to about 1/8-inch thickness.
- Using a round cookie cutter or drinking glass slightly larger than the muffin tin cups, cut out circles of dough to line the muffin cups.
- Gently press the dough circles into the muffin tin cups, ensuring they cover the bottom and sides.
- Fill each pastry-lined cup with a spoonful of the prepared mincemeat filling, filling them just below the rim.

4. Add Pastry Lids and Bake:

- Roll out the second portion of chilled pastry dough to 1/8-inch thickness. Cut out smaller circles or shapes to use as tops for the mince pies.
- Place the pastry lids over the filled mince pies, pressing the edges lightly to seal.
- Brush the tops of the pies with beaten egg wash for a golden finish.
- Use a sharp knife to make a small slit or cross on top of each pie to allow steam to escape during baking.
- Bake in the preheated oven for 20-25 minutes, or until the pastry is golden brown and cooked through.

5. Serve and Enjoy:

- Remove the mince pies from the muffin tin and let them cool slightly on a wire rack.
- Dust the cooled pies with powdered sugar before serving.
- Enjoy these delicious homemade mince pies warm or at room temperature, with a cup of tea or coffee.

Homemade mince pies are a delightful holiday treat that can be enjoyed throughout the festive season. They also make wonderful gifts when packaged beautifully. Share these traditional British pies with family and friends and savor the warm, spiced flavors of the season!

Red Velvet Cupcakes

Ingredients:

For the Cupcakes:

- 1 1/4 cups all-purpose flour
- 1/2 teaspoon baking soda
- 1/2 teaspoon salt
- 2 tablespoons unsweetened cocoa powder
- 1/2 cup unsalted butter, softened
- 1 cup granulated sugar
- 2 large eggs
- 1 teaspoon vanilla extract
- 1/2 cup buttermilk
- 1 tablespoon red food coloring (gel or liquid)
- 1 teaspoon white vinegar
- 1 teaspoon baking powder

For the Cream Cheese Frosting:

- 8 ounces cream cheese, softened
- 1/2 cup unsalted butter, softened
- 3-4 cups powdered sugar
- 1 teaspoon vanilla extract

Instructions:

1. Preheat Oven and Prepare Cupcake Pan:

- Preheat your oven to 350°F (175°C). Line a standard 12-cup muffin tin with cupcake liners.

2. Sift Dry Ingredients:

- In a medium bowl, sift together the flour, baking soda, salt, and cocoa powder. Set aside.

3. Cream Butter and Sugar:

- In a large mixing bowl, cream together the softened butter and granulated sugar until light and fluffy.

4. Add Eggs and Vanilla:

- Beat in the eggs, one at a time, until well combined. Stir in the vanilla extract.

5. Mix in Buttermilk and Red Food Coloring:

- In a small bowl, whisk together the buttermilk and red food coloring. Gradually add this mixture to the butter mixture, mixing until evenly incorporated.

6. Combine Wet and Dry Ingredients:

- Gradually add the sifted dry ingredients to the wet ingredients, mixing until just combined.

7. Add Vinegar and Baking Powder:

- In a small bowl, mix together the white vinegar and baking powder. Quickly fold this mixture into the cupcake batter until evenly distributed.

8. Fill Cupcake Liners:

- Divide the cupcake batter evenly among the prepared cupcake liners, filling each liner about 2/3 full.

9. Bake Cupcakes:

- Bake in the preheated oven for 18-20 minutes, or until a toothpick inserted into the center of a cupcake comes out clean.
- Remove the cupcakes from the oven and let them cool in the pan for a few minutes before transferring to a wire rack to cool completely.

10. Make Cream Cheese Frosting:

   - In a mixing bowl, beat together the softened cream cheese and butter until smooth and creamy.
   - Gradually add powdered sugar, 1 cup at a time, until the desired sweetness and consistency is reached.
   - Stir in the vanilla extract.

11. Frost Cupcakes:

   - Once the cupcakes are completely cooled, pipe or spread the cream cheese frosting onto the cupcakes using a piping bag or offset spatula.

12. Serve and Enjoy:

   - Enjoy these delicious homemade red velvet cupcakes! They are perfect for celebrating special occasions or simply indulging in a sweet treat.

These red velvet cupcakes with cream cheese frosting are sure to impress with their rich flavor and beautiful appearance. They are a favorite dessert that everyone will love!

Danish Butter Cookies

Ingredients:

- 1 cup unsalted butter, softened
- 1/2 cup granulated sugar
- 2 cups all-purpose flour
- 1/2 teaspoon salt
- 1 teaspoon vanilla extract
- 1 egg yolk
- Optional: Additional sugar for sprinkling on top

Instructions:

1. Preheat Oven and Prepare Baking Sheets:

- Preheat your oven to 350°F (175°C). Line baking sheets with parchment paper or silicone baking mats.

2. Cream Butter and Sugar:

- In a large mixing bowl, cream together the softened butter and granulated sugar until light and fluffy.

3. Add Vanilla and Egg Yolk:

- Mix in the vanilla extract and egg yolk until well combined.

4. Mix Dry Ingredients:

- In a separate bowl, whisk together the flour and salt.

5. Combine Wet and Dry Ingredients:

- Gradually add the flour mixture to the butter mixture, mixing until a dough forms. Be careful not to overmix.

6. Fill Cookie Press or Pastry Bag:

- Transfer the cookie dough to a cookie press fitted with desired shapes or to a pastry bag fitted with a large star tip.

7. Pipe Cookies onto Baking Sheets:

- Pipe the dough into desired shapes (such as S-shapes, circles, rosettes) onto the prepared baking sheets, leaving space between each cookie.

8. Optional: Sprinkle with Sugar:

- If desired, sprinkle the cookies with a little granulated sugar before baking for added sweetness and texture.

9. Bake Cookies:

- Bake in the preheated oven for 10-12 minutes, or until the edges of the cookies are lightly golden.

10. Cool and Store:

- Remove the cookies from the oven and let them cool on the baking sheets for a few minutes.
- Transfer the cookies to a wire rack to cool completely before serving or storing.

11. Enjoy:

- Serve these delicious Danish butter cookies with a cup of tea or coffee, or package them in a decorative tin for a thoughtful homemade gift.

These homemade Danish butter cookies are perfect for any occasion and are sure to be a hit with family and friends. Experiment with different shapes and decorations to make them extra special!

Hot Cross Buns

Ingredients:

For the Buns:

- 4 cups all-purpose flour
- 1/3 cup granulated sugar
- 1 teaspoon salt
- 1 tablespoon active dry yeast
- 1 1/4 cups warm milk (110°F / 45°C)
- 1/4 cup unsalted butter, melted
- 1 large egg
- 1/2 cup currants or raisins
- Zest of 1 orange (optional)
- 1 teaspoon ground cinnamon
- 1/4 teaspoon ground nutmeg
- 1/4 teaspoon ground cloves

For the Cross Paste:

- 1/2 cup all-purpose flour
- 5-6 tablespoons water

For the Glaze:

- 1/4 cup apricot preserves or orange marmalade
- 1 tablespoon water

Instructions:

1. Activate Yeast:

   - In a small bowl, dissolve 1 tablespoon of sugar in warm milk. Sprinkle yeast over the mixture and let it sit for 5-10 minutes until frothy.

2. Mix Dry Ingredients:

   - In a large mixing bowl, whisk together the flour, remaining sugar, salt, ground cinnamon, nutmeg, and cloves.

3. Combine Wet Ingredients:

- Make a well in the center of the dry ingredients. Pour in the yeast mixture, melted butter, and beaten egg. Mix until a dough forms.

4. Knead the Dough:

- Turn the dough out onto a floured surface and knead for 8-10 minutes until smooth and elastic. Alternatively, use a stand mixer with a dough hook attachment.

5. Add Currants/Raisins and Orange Zest:

- Flatten the dough and sprinkle currants/raisins and orange zest over it. Knead for another 2-3 minutes until the fruits are evenly distributed.

6. First Rise:

- Place the dough in a greased bowl, cover with a clean kitchen towel, and let it rise in a warm place for 1-1.5 hours or until doubled in size.

7. Shape the Buns:

- Punch down the risen dough and divide it into 12 equal portions. Shape each portion into a smooth round bun and place them on a parchment-lined baking sheet, leaving space between each bun.

8. Second Rise:

- Cover the buns with a clean kitchen towel and let them rise again in a warm place for 30-45 minutes until puffy.

9. Preheat Oven:

- Preheat your oven to 375°F (190°C).

10. Make the Cross Paste:

- In a small bowl, mix together the flour and water to form a thick paste. Transfer the paste into a piping bag or a small plastic bag with a corner snipped off.

11. Pipe the Crosses:

- Pipe a cross shape onto the top of each bun using the paste.

12. Bake the Buns:

- Bake the buns in the preheated oven for 15-18 minutes or until golden brown.

13. Make the Glaze:

- In a small saucepan, heat the apricot preserves or orange marmalade with water until melted and smooth.

14. Glaze the Buns:

- Brush the warm buns with the glaze as soon as they come out of the oven.

15. Serve and Enjoy:

- Let the hot cross buns cool slightly before serving. Enjoy them warm with butter, or split and toasted.

These homemade hot cross buns are wonderfully spiced and make a delightful Easter or anytime treat. They are best enjoyed fresh but can also be stored in an airtight container for a few days and reheated before serving. Enjoy sharing these delicious buns with family and friends!

Lebkuchen (German spiced cookies)

Ingredients:

For the Lebkuchen Cookies:

- 2 cups all-purpose flour
- 1/2 teaspoon baking powder
- 1/4 teaspoon baking soda
- 1 tablespoon ground cinnamon
- 1 teaspoon ground ginger
- 1/2 teaspoon ground cloves
- 1/2 teaspoon ground nutmeg
- 1/4 teaspoon ground allspice
- 1/4 teaspoon ground cardamom
- 1/4 teaspoon salt
- 1/2 cup unsalted butter, softened
- 1/2 cup granulated sugar
- 1/2 cup brown sugar, packed
- 1 large egg
- 1/2 cup honey
- 1/4 cup finely chopped candied citrus peel (optional)
- 1/4 cup finely chopped candied ginger (optional)
- 1/2 cup chopped almonds or hazelnuts (optional)

For the Glaze:

- 1 cup powdered sugar
- 2-3 tablespoons milk
- 1/2 teaspoon vanilla extract

Instructions:

1. Prepare the Dough:

- In a medium bowl, whisk together the flour, baking powder, baking soda, spices (cinnamon, ginger, cloves, nutmeg, allspice, cardamom), and salt. Set aside.

- In a large mixing bowl, cream together the softened butter, granulated sugar, and brown sugar until light and fluffy.
- Add the egg and honey to the butter mixture, and beat until well combined.
- Gradually add the dry flour mixture to the wet ingredients, mixing until a smooth dough forms.
- Fold in the optional chopped candied citrus peel, candied ginger, and chopped nuts, if using.

2. Chill the Dough:

- Wrap the dough in plastic wrap and chill in the refrigerator for at least 1 hour, or overnight.

3. Shape and Bake the Cookies:

- Preheat your oven to 350°F (175°C) and line baking sheets with parchment paper.
- Divide the chilled dough into portions and roll each portion into balls (about 1 inch in diameter). Place the balls onto the prepared baking sheets, spacing them about 2 inches apart.
- Flatten each ball slightly with your fingers or the back of a spoon to form round cookie shapes.
- Bake the cookies in the preheated oven for 10-12 minutes, or until the edges are lightly golden brown.

4. Make the Glaze:

- In a small bowl, whisk together the powdered sugar, milk, and vanilla extract until smooth and well combined. Adjust the consistency by adding more milk or powdered sugar as needed.

5. Glaze the Cookies:

- Allow the cookies to cool on the baking sheets for a few minutes, then transfer them to a wire rack to cool completely.
- Once the cookies are completely cool, drizzle the glaze over the tops using a spoon or a small piping bag.

6. Let the Glaze Set:

- Allow the glaze to set before serving or storing the cookies.

7. Serve and Enjoy:

- Enjoy these delicious homemade Lebkuchen cookies with a cup of tea or coffee, or package them in festive boxes or tins for gifting during the holidays.

These Lebkuchen cookies are wonderfully aromatic and full of warm spices, making them a perfect holiday treat. Customize them with your favorite additions like candied peel or nuts, and enjoy the festive flavors of traditional German baking!

Chocolate Peppermint Bark Cookies

Ingredients:

For the Cookies:

- 1 cup all-purpose flour
- 1/3 cup unsweetened cocoa powder
- 1/2 teaspoon baking soda
- 1/4 teaspoon salt
- 1/2 cup unsalted butter, softened
- 1/2 cup granulated sugar
- 1/2 cup brown sugar, packed
- 1 large egg
- 1 teaspoon vanilla extract
- 1/2 cup dark chocolate chips or chunks
- Crushed peppermint candies or candy canes, for topping

For the Peppermint Bark Topping:

- 8 ounces semi-sweet or dark chocolate, chopped
- 1/2 teaspoon peppermint extract
- 4-6 candy canes or peppermint candies, crushed

Instructions:

1. Preheat Oven:

- Preheat your oven to 350°F (175°C). Line baking sheets with parchment paper.

2. Prepare Cookie Dough:

- In a medium bowl, whisk together the flour, cocoa powder, baking soda, and salt. Set aside.
- In a large mixing bowl, cream together the softened butter, granulated sugar, and brown sugar until light and fluffy.
- Add the egg and vanilla extract to the butter mixture, and beat until well combined.
- Gradually add the dry flour mixture to the wet ingredients, mixing until a soft dough forms.

- Fold in the dark chocolate chips or chunks until evenly distributed.

3. Shape and Bake Cookies:

    - Drop tablespoonfuls of cookie dough onto the prepared baking sheets, spacing them about 2 inches apart.
    - Flatten each cookie slightly with your fingers or the back of a spoon.
    - Bake in the preheated oven for 10-12 minutes, or until the edges are set. The cookies will be soft.
    - Remove from the oven and let the cookies cool on the baking sheets for a few minutes before transferring them to a wire rack to cool completely.

4. Prepare Peppermint Bark Topping:

    - In a heatproof bowl set over a pot of simmering water (double boiler method), melt the chopped semi-sweet or dark chocolate, stirring until smooth.
    - Stir in the peppermint extract until well combined.

5. Assemble the Cookies:

    - Dip the top of each cooled cookie into the melted chocolate peppermint mixture, allowing any excess chocolate to drip off.
    - Place the dipped cookies back onto the parchment-lined baking sheets.
    - Immediately sprinkle crushed peppermint candies or candy cane pieces over the chocolate topping.

6. Let the Chocolate Set:

    - Allow the chocolate topping to set at room temperature, or place the cookies in the refrigerator for faster setting.

7. Serve and Enjoy:

    - Once the chocolate peppermint bark topping is set, serve these delicious cookies and enjoy the festive flavors!

These chocolate peppermint bark cookies are a delightful combination of chocolatey, minty, and crunchy goodness. They make wonderful holiday treats and are sure to be a hit with family and friends. Store any leftover cookies in an airtight container at room temperature for several days. Enjoy!

Coconut Macaroons

Ingredients:

- 4 large egg whites
- 1/2 cup granulated sugar
- 1/2 teaspoon vanilla extract
- 1/4 teaspoon almond extract (optional)
- 1/4 teaspoon salt
- 3 cups sweetened shredded coconut
- Optional: Melted chocolate for drizzling or dipping (semisweet, milk, or white chocolate)

Instructions:

1. Preheat Oven:

- Preheat your oven to 325°F (160°C). Line baking sheets with parchment paper or silicone baking mats.

2. Prepare the Coconut Mixture:

- In a large heatproof bowl, whisk together the egg whites, granulated sugar, vanilla extract, almond extract (if using), and salt.
- Place the bowl over a pot of simmering water (double boiler method) and whisk constantly until the sugar has dissolved and the mixture is slightly warm to the touch, about 2-3 minutes. Be careful not to cook the egg whites.

3. Mix in Shredded Coconut:

- Remove the bowl from the heat. Stir in the shredded coconut until well combined and evenly coated with the egg white mixture.

4. Shape the Macaroons:

- Using a spoon or cookie scoop, portion out the coconut mixture and drop onto the prepared baking sheets, leaving space between each macaroon.

- You can use a small ice cream scoop or tablespoon to form the macaroons. They can also be shaped with your hands into mounds if desired.

5. Bake the Macaroons:

- Bake in the preheated oven for 20-25 minutes, or until the edges of the macaroons are golden brown.

6. Optional Chocolate Drizzle or Dip:

- If desired, melt chocolate of your choice (semisweet, milk, or white chocolate) in a heatproof bowl set over a pot of simmering water (double boiler method) or in the microwave.
- Drizzle the melted chocolate over the cooled macaroons using a spoon or fork, or dip the bottoms of the macaroons into the melted chocolate.

7. Let the Macaroons Cool:

- Allow the macaroons to cool completely on the baking sheets before serving or storing.

8. Serve and Enjoy:

- Once the chocolate has set (if using), serve these delicious coconut macaroons and enjoy their chewy texture and sweet coconut flavor!

These homemade coconut macaroons are simple to make and perfect for sharing with family and friends. They can be stored in an airtight container at room temperature for several days. Enjoy these delightful treats as a sweet snack or dessert!

Cranberry Pistachio Biscotti

Ingredients:

- 2 cups all-purpose flour
- 1 teaspoon baking powder
- 1/4 teaspoon salt
- 1/2 cup unsalted butter, softened
- 3/4 cup granulated sugar
- 2 large eggs
- 1 teaspoon vanilla extract
- 1/2 cup dried cranberries
- 1/2 cup shelled pistachios, coarsely chopped
- Zest of 1 orange (optional)
- 1 egg white (for brushing)

Instructions:

1. Preheat Oven:

    - Preheat your oven to 350°F (175°C). Line a baking sheet with parchment paper or a silicone baking mat.

2. Mix Dry Ingredients:

    - In a medium bowl, whisk together the flour, baking powder, and salt. Set aside.

3. Cream Butter and Sugar:

    - In a large mixing bowl, cream together the softened butter and granulated sugar until light and fluffy.

4. Add Eggs and Vanilla:

    - Beat in the eggs, one at a time, until well combined. Stir in the vanilla extract.

5. Combine Wet and Dry Ingredients:

- Gradually add the dry flour mixture to the wet ingredients, mixing until just combined.

6. Add Cranberries, Pistachios, and Orange Zest:

- Fold in the dried cranberries, chopped pistachios, and orange zest (if using) until evenly distributed in the dough.

7. Shape the Dough:

- Divide the dough in half. On a lightly floured surface, shape each portion of dough into a log about 12 inches long and 2 inches wide.

8. Brush with Egg White:

- Place the logs on the prepared baking sheet, spaced a few inches apart. Brush the tops and sides of the logs with beaten egg white.

9. Bake the Logs:

- Bake in the preheated oven for 25-30 minutes, or until the logs are lightly golden and firm to the touch.

10. Cool and Slice:

- Remove the baking sheet from the oven and let the logs cool for 10-15 minutes. Reduce the oven temperature to 325°F (160°C).
- Transfer the cooled logs to a cutting board. Using a sharp knife, slice the logs diagonally into 1/2-inch thick slices.

11. Second Bake:

- Arrange the biscotti slices cut side down on the baking sheet. Return to the oven and bake for an additional 10-12 minutes, or until the biscotti are crisp and golden brown.

12. Cool Completely:

- Remove the biscotti from the oven and let them cool completely on a wire rack.

13. Serve and Enjoy:

- Once cooled, serve these delicious cranberry pistachio biscotti with coffee, tea, or as a sweet snack.

These homemade biscotti can be stored in an airtight container at room temperature for up to two weeks. Enjoy the festive flavors of cranberry and pistachio in this crunchy and satisfying cookie!

Snowflake Shortbread Cookies

Ingredients:

- 1 cup unsalted butter, softened
- 1/2 cup powdered sugar
- 2 cups all-purpose flour
- 1/4 teaspoon salt
- 1 teaspoon vanilla extract
- Optional: Decorative icing, colored sugar, or sprinkles for decorating

Instructions:

1. Preheat Oven:

- Preheat your oven to 350°F (175°C). Line baking sheets with parchment paper.

2. Cream Butter and Sugar:

- In a large mixing bowl, cream together the softened butter and powdered sugar until light and fluffy.

3. Mix in Flour and Salt:

- Gradually add the flour and salt to the butter mixture, mixing until the dough comes together. Add the vanilla extract and mix until incorporated.

4. Roll Out the Dough:

- Transfer the dough onto a lightly floured surface. Roll out the dough to about 1/4-inch thickness.

5. Cut Out Snowflake Shapes:

- Use snowflake-shaped cookie cutters to cut out cookies from the rolled dough. Place the cut-out cookies onto the prepared baking sheets, spacing them about 1 inch apart.

6. Chill the Cookies:

- Place the baking sheets with the cut-out cookies in the refrigerator for about 15-20 minutes to chill the dough. Chilled dough helps the cookies maintain their shape during baking.

7. Bake the Cookies:

- Bake the chilled cookies in the preheated oven for 10-12 minutes, or until the edges are lightly golden. Be careful not to over-bake.

8. Cool the Cookies:

- Remove the baking sheets from the oven and let the cookies cool on the sheets for a few minutes before transferring them to a wire rack to cool completely.

9. Decorate (Optional):

- Once the cookies are completely cooled, you can decorate them with icing, colored sugar, or sprinkles. Use piping bags or small brushes to add decorative details.

10. Serve and Enjoy:

- Allow the icing or decorations to set before serving these delightful snowflake shortbread cookies.

These homemade snowflake shortbread cookies are perfect for winter gatherings, holiday parties, or as a sweet gift. Enjoy the buttery flavor and delicate texture of these festive treats! Store any leftover cookies in an airtight container at room temperature for several days.

Caramel Pecan Turtle Clusters

Ingredients:

- 1 cup pecan halves
- 24 soft caramel candies, unwrapped
- 1 tablespoon heavy cream
- 8 ounces semisweet or milk chocolate, chopped (or use chocolate chips)
- Sea salt flakes, for garnish (optional)

Instructions:

1. Prepare Pecan Clusters:

- Line a baking sheet with parchment paper or a silicone baking mat. Arrange pecan halves into clusters of 3-4 nuts each on the prepared baking sheet. Leave some space between each cluster.

2. Melt Caramel:

- In a microwave-safe bowl, combine the unwrapped caramel candies and heavy cream. Microwave in 30-second intervals, stirring in between, until the caramel is melted and smooth. Be careful not to overheat.

3. Top Pecans with Caramel:

- Spoon a dollop of melted caramel over each pecan cluster on the baking sheet. Use the back of the spoon to spread the caramel slightly.

4. Cool the Caramel:

- Allow the caramel-topped pecan clusters to cool and set at room temperature for about 30 minutes, or until the caramel is firm.

5. Melt Chocolate:

- In another microwave-safe bowl, melt the chopped chocolate in 30-second intervals, stirring in between, until smooth and melted.

6. Coat Pecan Clusters with Chocolate:

- Spoon melted chocolate over each caramel-topped pecan cluster, covering the caramel and pecans completely.

7. Garnish (Optional):

- While the chocolate is still wet, sprinkle a pinch of sea salt flakes over each cluster for a delicious salty-sweet contrast.

8. Set and Serve:

- Allow the chocolate to set completely at room temperature or in the refrigerator until firm.

9. Enjoy:

- Once the chocolate is set, carefully peel the clusters off the parchment paper or baking mat.
- Serve these delicious caramel pecan turtle clusters as a delightful treat or gift for special occasions.

Tips:

- Store the caramel pecan turtle clusters in an airtight container at room temperature for up to one week. Layer the clusters with parchment paper to prevent sticking.
- Customize the recipe by using different types of nuts, such as almonds or walnuts, and adding extra toppings like drizzled white chocolate or sprinkles.

These homemade caramel pecan turtle clusters are rich, sweet, and absolutely irresistible. Enjoy the combination of creamy caramel, crunchy pecans, and smooth chocolate in each delightful bite!

Chocolate Covered Pretzels

Ingredients:

- Pretzel twists or rods
- 8 ounces (about 1 1/3 cups) of chocolate chips (milk, dark, or white chocolate)
- Optional: Additional toppings like sprinkles, chopped nuts, or sea salt flakes

Instructions:

1. Prepare the Pretzels:

- Line a baking sheet with parchment paper or wax paper.

2. Melt the Chocolate:

- Place the chocolate chips in a microwave-safe bowl. Microwave in 30-second intervals, stirring in between, until the chocolate is completely melted and smooth. Be careful not to overheat the chocolate.

3. Dip the Pretzels:

- Using a fork or dipping tool, dip each pretzel into the melted chocolate, coating it completely. Allow any excess chocolate to drip back into the bowl.

4. Place on Baking Sheet:

- Place the chocolate-coated pretzels on the prepared baking sheet, spacing them apart to avoid sticking together.

5. Add Toppings (Optional):

- While the chocolate is still wet, sprinkle your desired toppings over the pretzels. You can use sprinkles, chopped nuts, or a pinch of sea salt flakes for a sweet-salty flavor contrast.

6. Let the Chocolate Set:

- Allow the chocolate-covered pretzels to set at room temperature until the chocolate hardens and becomes firm. You can also place the baking sheet in the refrigerator for faster setting.

7. Serve and Enjoy:

- Once the chocolate is completely set, gently peel the pretzels off the parchment paper.
- Serve these delicious homemade chocolate-covered pretzels as a snack or dessert. They are also great for packaging in gift bags or boxes for special occasions.

Tips:

- Experiment with different types of chocolate (milk, dark, or white) or even flavored chocolate chips (such as mint or peanut butter) for variety.
- For a festive touch, use colored sprinkles or seasonal decorations to customize your chocolate-covered pretzels for holidays or special events.
- Store any leftover chocolate-covered pretzels in an airtight container at room temperature. They should stay fresh for several days, although they are best enjoyed within a few days of making.

These homemade chocolate-covered pretzels are quick to make and always a crowd-pleaser. Enjoy the irresistible combination of salty pretzels and sweet chocolate in every bite!

Cinnamon Sugar Palmiers

Ingredients:

- 1 sheet puff pastry (store-bought, thawed if frozen)
- 1/2 cup granulated sugar
- 1 tablespoon ground cinnamon
- Pinch of salt
- Optional: 1/4 teaspoon ground nutmeg or cardamom (for extra flavor)

Instructions:

1. Preheat Oven:

- Preheat your oven to 400°F (200°C). Line a baking sheet with parchment paper or a silicone baking mat.

2. Prepare Cinnamon Sugar Mixture:

- In a small bowl, mix together the granulated sugar, ground cinnamon, salt, and optional ground nutmeg or cardamom. Set aside.

3. Roll Out Puff Pastry:

- On a lightly floured surface, roll out the puff pastry sheet into a rectangle, about 12x10 inches in size.

4. Spread Cinnamon Sugar:

- Sprinkle half of the cinnamon sugar mixture evenly over the puff pastry sheet, covering the entire surface.

5. Fold the Edges:

- Starting from the long edges, fold each side of the puff pastry towards the center until they meet in the middle.

6. Fold Again:

   - Fold one half of the pastry over the other half, like closing a book.

7. Slice Palmiers:

   - Using a sharp knife, slice the folded pastry into 1/2-inch thick slices. You should get about 12-14 slices.

8. Coat with Cinnamon Sugar:

   - Dip each slice into the remaining cinnamon sugar mixture, coating both sides generously.

9. Arrange on Baking Sheet:

   - Place the coated palmiers onto the prepared baking sheet, spacing them about 2 inches apart.

10. Bake:

    - Bake in the preheated oven for 15-18 minutes, or until the palmiers are golden brown and crispy.

11. Cool and Serve:

    - Remove the baked cinnamon sugar palmiers from the oven and let them cool on the baking sheet for a few minutes.
    - Transfer the palmiers to a wire rack to cool completely before serving.

12. Enjoy:

    - Serve these delicious homemade cinnamon sugar palmiers with coffee, tea, or as a sweet snack.

Tips:

- You can customize these palmiers by adding chopped nuts (such as almonds or pecans) or a drizzle of melted chocolate on top after baking.
- Store any leftover cinnamon sugar palmiers in an airtight container at room temperature. They are best enjoyed fresh but will keep for a few days.

These cinnamon sugar palmiers are simple to make yet impressive in flavor and appearance. Enjoy the delightful combination of crispy puff pastry and sweet cinnamon sugar in every bite!

Lemon Bars

Ingredients:

For the Shortbread Crust:

- 1 cup (2 sticks) unsalted butter, softened
- 1/2 cup granulated sugar
- 2 cups all-purpose flour
- 1/4 teaspoon salt

For the Lemon Filling:

- 1 1/2 cups granulated sugar
- 1/4 cup all-purpose flour
- 4 large eggs
- 2/3 cup freshly squeezed lemon juice (from about 3-4 lemons)
- Zest of 1 lemon
- Powdered sugar, for dusting (optional)

Instructions:

1. Preheat Oven and Prepare Pan:

   - Preheat your oven to 350°F (175°C). Grease a 9x13-inch baking pan or line it with parchment paper, leaving an overhang for easy removal.

2. Make the Shortbread Crust:

   - In a large mixing bowl, cream together the softened butter and granulated sugar until light and fluffy.
   - Add the flour and salt to the butter mixture, and mix until crumbly and combined.
   - Press the mixture evenly into the bottom of the prepared baking pan.

3. Bake the Crust:

   - Bake the crust in the preheated oven for 15-20 minutes, or until lightly golden brown around the edges. Remove from the oven and set aside.

4. Prepare the Lemon Filling:

- In a separate bowl, whisk together the granulated sugar and flour.
- Add the eggs, lemon juice, and lemon zest to the sugar mixture, and whisk until smooth and well combined.

5. Pour Lemon Filling Over Crust:

- Pour the lemon filling over the baked crust in the pan.

6. Bake the Lemon Bars:

- Return the pan to the oven and bake for 20-25 minutes, or until the filling is set and the edges are lightly golden brown.

7. Cool and Chill:

- Remove the pan from the oven and let the lemon bars cool completely in the pan on a wire rack.
- Once cooled, refrigerate the lemon bars for at least 2 hours (or overnight) to allow them to set and firm up.

8. Slice and Serve:

- Use the parchment paper overhang to lift the chilled lemon bars out of the pan. Place them on a cutting board and slice into squares or rectangles.
- Dust the tops with powdered sugar before serving, if desired.

9. Enjoy:

- Serve these delicious homemade lemon bars chilled or at room temperature. They are a refreshing and delightful dessert!

Tips:

- For extra lemon flavor, you can add more lemon zest to the filling or sprinkle some zest on top before serving.
- Store leftover lemon bars in an airtight container in the refrigerator for up to 3-4 days. Bring them to room temperature before serving.

These homemade lemon bars are a perfect balance of sweet and tangy, with a buttery crust that complements the bright lemon filling. They are sure to be a hit at any occasion!

Chocolate Truffles

Ingredients:

- 8 ounces (about 1 1/3 cups) good quality semi-sweet or dark chocolate, finely chopped
- 1/2 cup heavy cream
- 1 teaspoon vanilla extract
- Optional flavorings (such as liqueur, espresso, or spices)
- Coating options: cocoa powder, powdered sugar, chopped nuts, shredded coconut, or melted chocolate for dipping

Instructions:

1. Prepare the Chocolate Ganache:

- Place the chopped chocolate in a heatproof bowl.
- In a small saucepan, heat the heavy cream over medium heat until it just begins to simmer (small bubbles form around the edges of the pan).
- Pour the hot cream over the chopped chocolate. Let it sit undisturbed for 1-2 minutes to soften the chocolate.
- Gently whisk the mixture together until smooth and glossy. If needed, you can place the bowl over a pot of simmering water (double boiler) and continue stirring until completely melted and smooth.
- Stir in the vanilla extract and any optional flavorings (such as a tablespoon of liqueur or a dash of espresso powder).

2. Chill the Ganache:

- Cover the bowl with plastic wrap, pressing it directly onto the surface of the ganache to prevent a skin from forming.
- Refrigerate the ganache until firm, about 2-3 hours or overnight.

3. Shape the Truffles:

- Once the ganache is firm, use a small spoon or melon baller to scoop out small portions of ganache.

- Quickly roll each portion between your palms to form smooth balls. Work quickly to prevent the ganache from melting too much.

4. Coat the Truffles:

- Roll each truffle in your desired coating. Some popular options include cocoa powder, powdered sugar, chopped nuts, shredded coconut, or even dipped in melted chocolate.
- Place the coated truffles on a baking sheet lined with parchment paper.

5. Chill and Serve:

- Refrigerate the truffles for at least 30 minutes to set the coating and firm up the truffles.
- Once chilled, arrange the truffles in mini cupcake liners or on a serving dish.

6. Enjoy:

- Serve these delightful homemade chocolate truffles as a sweet treat or gift. They are best enjoyed at room temperature.

Tips:

- Experiment with different coatings and flavorings to customize your chocolate truffles. For a boozy twist, try adding a splash of rum, brandy, or flavored liqueur to the ganache.
- Store the chocolate truffles in an airtight container in the refrigerator for up to two weeks. Bring them to room temperature before serving for the best flavor and texture.

These homemade chocolate truffles are rich, creamy, and irresistible. Enjoy the indulgent experience of biting into these silky-smooth treats!

Holiday Thumbprint Cookies

Ingredients:

- 1 cup (2 sticks) unsalted butter, softened
- 2/3 cup granulated sugar
- 1 teaspoon vanilla extract
- 2 cups all-purpose flour
- 1/2 teaspoon salt
- 1/2 cup jam or preserves (choose your favorite flavor)
- Festive sprinkles or powdered sugar, for decorating (optional)

Instructions:

1. Preheat Oven:

- Preheat your oven to 350°F (175°C). Line baking sheets with parchment paper or silicone baking mats.

2. Cream Butter and Sugar:

- In a large mixing bowl, cream together the softened butter and granulated sugar until light and fluffy.

3. Add Vanilla and Dry Ingredients:

- Mix in the vanilla extract.
- Gradually add the flour and salt to the butter mixture, mixing until the dough comes together and forms a soft ball.

4. Shape the Cookies:

- Roll tablespoonfuls of dough into balls and place them on the prepared baking sheets, spacing them about 1 inch apart.

5. Make Thumbprint Indentations:

- Use your thumb or the back of a small spoon to make indentations in the center of each cookie. The indentations should be deep enough to hold the filling but not go all the way through the dough.

6. Fill the Thumbprints:

- Spoon about 1/2 teaspoon of jam or preserves into each indentation. You can use one type of jam or mix and match flavors for variety.

7. Decorate (Optional):

- If desired, sprinkle festive sprinkles or powdered sugar over the filled thumbprints for a decorative touch.

8. Bake the Cookies:

- Bake in the preheated oven for 10-12 minutes, or until the edges of the cookies are lightly golden.

9. Cool and Serve:

- Remove the cookies from the oven and let them cool on the baking sheets for a few minutes before transferring them to a wire rack to cool completely.

10. Enjoy:

- Serve these delightful homemade holiday thumbprint cookies as a festive treat for parties, cookie exchanges, or holiday gatherings.

Tips:

- Experiment with different flavors of jam or preserves to create a variety of thumbprint cookies. Raspberry, strawberry, apricot, and cherry are popular choices.
- To make the cookies more festive, use colored sugar or holiday-themed sprinkles for decorating.

- Store the cooled cookies in an airtight container at room temperature for up to one week. The cookies can also be frozen for longer storage.

These holiday thumbprint cookies are simple to make and always a hit with family and friends. Enjoy the buttery cookie base and fruity jam filling in every delightful bite!

Cherry Almond Bread

Ingredients:

- 1/2 cup unsalted butter, softened
- 1 cup granulated sugar
- 2 large eggs
- 1 teaspoon almond extract
- 2 cups all-purpose flour
- 1 teaspoon baking powder
- 1/2 teaspoon baking soda
- 1/2 teaspoon salt
- 1 cup buttermilk
- 1 1/2 cups fresh or frozen cherries, pitted and chopped
- 1/2 cup sliced almonds

For the Glaze (optional):

- 1 cup powdered sugar
- 1-2 tablespoons milk or almond milk
- 1/2 teaspoon almond extract

Instructions:

1. Preheat Oven and Prepare Pan:

   - Preheat your oven to 350°F (175°C). Grease and flour a 9x5-inch loaf pan or line it with parchment paper.

2. Cream Butter and Sugar:

   - In a large mixing bowl, cream together the softened butter and granulated sugar until light and fluffy.

3. Add Eggs and Almond Extract:

   - Beat in the eggs, one at a time, until well combined. Stir in the almond extract.

4. Mix Dry Ingredients:

- In a separate bowl, whisk together the flour, baking powder, baking soda, and salt.

5. Combine Wet and Dry Ingredients:

    - Gradually add the dry flour mixture to the wet ingredients, alternating with buttermilk, beginning and ending with the flour mixture. Mix until just combined.

6. Fold in Cherries and Almonds:

    - Gently fold in the chopped cherries and sliced almonds into the batter, reserving some almonds for topping if desired.

7. Bake the Bread:

    - Pour the batter into the prepared loaf pan and spread it evenly.
    - If desired, sprinkle additional sliced almonds on top of the batter.
    - Bake in the preheated oven for 50-60 minutes, or until a toothpick inserted into the center comes out clean.

8. Cool and Glaze (optional):

    - Remove the bread from the oven and let it cool in the pan for about 10 minutes before transferring it to a wire rack to cool completely.
    - If making the glaze, whisk together the powdered sugar, milk or almond milk, and almond extract until smooth. Drizzle the glaze over the cooled bread.

9. Slice and Serve:

    - Once the glaze has set (if using), slice the cherry almond bread and serve.

10. Enjoy:

    - Enjoy this delicious homemade cherry almond bread as a delightful breakfast or snack.

Tips:

- If using frozen cherries, thaw and drain them well before chopping and adding to the batter.

- You can substitute the buttermilk with plain yogurt or sour cream for a tangy flavor.
- Store any leftover cherry almond bread in an airtight container at room temperature for up to 3 days, or refrigerate for longer storage. Warm slices in the microwave or toaster oven before serving, if desired.

This cherry almond bread is moist, flavorful, and packed with the delicious combination of cherries and almonds. It's a wonderful treat to enjoy during any season!

Irish Cream Brownies

Ingredients:

- 1/2 cup (1 stick) unsalted butter
- 8 ounces semi-sweet chocolate, chopped
- 1 cup granulated sugar
- 2 large eggs
- 1/4 cup Irish Cream liqueur (e.g., Baileys)
- 1 teaspoon vanilla extract
- 1/2 cup all-purpose flour
- 1/4 teaspoon salt
- Optional: Powdered sugar or cocoa powder for dusting

Instructions:

1. Preheat Oven and Prepare Pan:

- Preheat your oven to 350°F (175°C). Grease and line an 8x8-inch baking pan with parchment paper, leaving an overhang for easy removal.

2. Melt Butter and Chocolate:

- In a medium saucepan, melt the butter and chopped chocolate over low heat, stirring frequently until smooth and melted. Remove from heat.

3. Mix Sugar, Eggs, and Liqueur:

- In a large mixing bowl, whisk together the granulated sugar, eggs, Irish Cream liqueur, and vanilla extract until well combined.

4. Combine Wet and Dry Ingredients:

- Gradually add the melted chocolate mixture to the egg mixture, stirring until smooth.
- Add the flour and salt to the batter, and fold gently until just combined. Be careful not to overmix.

5. Bake the Brownies:

- Pour the brownie batter into the prepared baking pan and spread it evenly.
- Bake in the preheated oven for 25-30 minutes, or until a toothpick inserted into the center comes out with a few moist crumbs. The brownies should be set but still fudgy.

6. Cool and Serve:

- Allow the brownies to cool completely in the pan on a wire rack.
- Once cooled, lift the brownies out of the pan using the parchment paper overhang. Transfer to a cutting board and cut into squares.

7. Dust (Optional):

- Dust the tops of the brownies with powdered sugar or cocoa powder before serving for a decorative touch.

8. Enjoy:

- Serve these delicious homemade Irish Cream brownies as a decadent dessert or treat.

Tips:

- For extra richness, you can add chopped nuts (such as walnuts or pecans) to the brownie batter before baking.
- If you prefer a non-alcoholic version, you can substitute the Irish Cream liqueur with an equal amount of milk or cream, and add a splash of coffee extract or additional vanilla extract for flavor.
- Store leftover brownies in an airtight container at room temperature for up to 3-4 days, or refrigerate for longer storage. Warm individual brownie squares in the microwave for a few seconds before serving, if desired.

These Irish Cream brownies are sure to be a hit with chocolate lovers and fans of Irish Cream liqueur. Enjoy the rich, fudgy texture and decadent flavor of these delightful treats!

Candy Cane Marshmallow Pops

Ingredients:

- Large marshmallows
- Candy canes
- White chocolate or candy melts
- Crushed candy canes or holiday sprinkles (for decorating)
- Lollipop sticks or skewers

Instructions:

1. Prepare Candy Canes:

    - Unwrap candy canes and place them in a plastic bag. Use a rolling pin or mallet to crush the candy canes into small pieces. Set aside.

2. Skewer Marshmallows:

    - Insert a lollipop stick or skewer into each marshmallow. Push it about halfway through the marshmallow, leaving enough space to hold onto the stick.

3. Melt White Chocolate:

    - In a microwave-safe bowl, melt the white chocolate or candy melts according to the package instructions. Stir until smooth and creamy.

4. Dip Marshmallows:

    - Dip each marshmallow into the melted white chocolate, covering it completely. Allow any excess chocolate to drip back into the bowl.

5. Decorate with Candy Canes:

    - Immediately sprinkle the crushed candy canes or holiday sprinkles over the melted chocolate before it hardens. This adds a festive touch and helps the decorations stick to the marshmallows.

6. Let the Chocolate Set:

- Place the candy cane marshmallow pops on a parchment-lined baking sheet or stand them upright in a glass or styrofoam block to allow the chocolate to set.

7. Serve or Gift:

- Once the chocolate is completely set and firm, your Candy Cane Marshmallow Pops are ready to serve! They make delightful holiday treats for parties or gifts for friends and family.

Tips:

- You can customize these marshmallow pops by using different flavors of marshmallows (such as vanilla or peppermint-flavored) and using dark or milk chocolate instead of white chocolate.
- Experiment with various decorations like crushed peppermint candies, colored sugar, or edible glitter for different looks.
- Wrap each Candy Cane Marshmallow Pop in cellophane or place them in treat bags tied with festive ribbons for beautiful holiday gifts.

These Candy Cane Marshmallow Pops are simple to make and bring a festive flair to any holiday celebration. Enjoy the combination of sweet marshmallows, creamy white chocolate, and crunchy candy cane pieces in each delicious bite!

Cranberry Bliss Bars

Ingredients:

For the Blondie Base:

- 1 cup (2 sticks) unsalted butter, melted
- 1 cup light brown sugar, packed
- 1/2 cup granulated sugar
- 2 large eggs
- 1 teaspoon vanilla extract
- 2 cups all-purpose flour
- 1/2 teaspoon baking powder
- 1/4 teaspoon salt
- 1/2 cup dried cranberries
- 1/2 cup white chocolate chips or chunks

For the Cream Cheese Frosting:

- 8 ounces cream cheese, softened
- 1 cup powdered sugar
- 1 teaspoon vanilla extract
- 1/2 cup dried cranberries, chopped

For Garnish:

- Additional white chocolate chips, melted (optional)
- Additional dried cranberries, chopped (optional)

Instructions:

1. Preheat Oven and Prepare Pan:

- Preheat your oven to 350°F (175°C). Grease a 9x13-inch baking pan or line it with parchment paper.

2. Make the Blondie Base:

- In a large mixing bowl, whisk together the melted butter, brown sugar, and granulated sugar until well combined.
- Add the eggs and vanilla extract, and whisk until smooth.
- Stir in the flour, baking powder, and salt until just combined.
- Fold in the dried cranberries and white chocolate chips.

3. Bake the Blondie Base:

- Spread the blondie batter evenly into the prepared baking pan.
- Bake in the preheated oven for 20-25 minutes, or until the edges are golden brown and a toothpick inserted into the center comes out clean.
- Remove from the oven and let the blondie base cool completely in the pan on a wire rack.

4. Make the Cream Cheese Frosting:

- In a mixing bowl, beat the softened cream cheese until smooth and creamy.
- Add the powdered sugar and vanilla extract, and beat until smooth and well combined.
- Stir in the chopped dried cranberries.

5. Frost and Decorate the Bars:

- Once the blondie base has cooled completely, spread the cream cheese frosting evenly over the top using an offset spatula.
- Optional: Drizzle melted white chocolate over the frosting and sprinkle with additional chopped dried cranberries for decoration.

6. Chill and Slice:

- Refrigerate the bars for at least 1 hour to allow the frosting to set.
- Once chilled, use a sharp knife to slice the Cranberry Bliss Bars into squares or rectangles.

7. Serve and Enjoy:

- Serve these delightful homemade Cranberry Bliss Bars chilled or at room temperature. They make a perfect holiday dessert or sweet treat for any occasion!

Tips:

- For best results, allow the bars to chill in the refrigerator before slicing to ensure clean cuts and neat presentation.
- Customize the recipe by adding chopped nuts (such as pecans or walnuts) to the blondie base for extra crunch and flavor.
- Store leftover Cranberry Bliss Bars in an airtight container in the refrigerator for up to 5 days. Bring them to room temperature before serving for the best texture and flavor.

These homemade Cranberry Bliss Bars are a wonderful addition to your holiday baking repertoire. Enjoy the festive flavors of cranberries and white chocolate in these delicious dessert bars!

Apricot Rugelach

Ingredients:

For the Dough:

- 1 cup (2 sticks) unsalted butter, softened
- 8 ounces cream cheese, softened
- 1/4 cup granulated sugar
- 2 cups all-purpose flour
- 1/4 teaspoon salt

For the Filling:

- 3/4 cup apricot preserves
- 1/2 cup finely chopped walnuts or pecans
- 1/4 cup granulated sugar
- 1 teaspoon ground cinnamon

For Assembly:

- 1 egg, beaten (for egg wash)
- Granulated sugar (for sprinkling)

Instructions:

1. Make the Dough:

- In a large mixing bowl, beat together the softened butter, cream cheese, and sugar until smooth and creamy.
- Add the flour and salt to the butter mixture, and mix until a dough forms. Divide the dough into 4 equal portions, shape each portion into a disk, and wrap them in plastic wrap. Chill the dough in the refrigerator for at least 1 hour or overnight.

2. Prepare the Filling:

- In a small bowl, mix together the apricot preserves, chopped nuts, sugar, and cinnamon until well combined. Set aside.

3. Roll Out the Dough:

- Preheat your oven to 350°F (175°C). Line baking sheets with parchment paper.
- On a lightly floured surface, roll out one disk of dough into a 9-inch circle. Spread about 3 tablespoons of the apricot filling evenly over the dough circle.
- Use a pizza cutter or sharp knife to cut the dough circle into 12 equal wedges, like a pizza.

4. Roll Up the Rugelach:

- Starting from the wide end, roll up each wedge of dough to form a crescent shape. Place the rugelach point-side down on the prepared baking sheets, spacing them about 1 inch apart.

5. Egg Wash and Sugar Topping:

- Brush the tops of the rugelach with beaten egg and sprinkle with granulated sugar.

6. Bake the Rugelach:

- Bake in the preheated oven for 20-25 minutes, or until golden brown and cooked through.

7. Cool and Serve:

- Remove the apricot rugelach from the oven and let them cool on the baking sheets for a few minutes before transferring them to a wire rack to cool completely.

8. Enjoy:

- Serve these delicious homemade apricot rugelach as a delightful treat for dessert, brunch, or snack time.

Tips:

- Feel free to substitute apricot preserves with other fruit preserves or jams, such as raspberry or strawberry, for different flavor variations.
- Store leftover apricot rugelach in an airtight container at room temperature for up to 3-4 days. They can also be frozen for longer storage.

These apricot rugelach are buttery, flaky, and filled with sweet fruit and nut filling. They make a wonderful addition to your holiday baking or anytime you want to enjoy a special homemade treat!

Maple Pecan Pie

Ingredients:

For the Pie Crust:

- 1 1/4 cups all-purpose flour
- 1/2 teaspoon salt
- 1/2 cup unsalted butter, chilled and cut into small cubes
- 3-4 tablespoons ice water

For the Filling:

- 1 cup pure maple syrup
- 3/4 cup light brown sugar, packed
- 1/4 cup unsalted butter, melted
- 3 large eggs, lightly beaten
- 1 teaspoon vanilla extract
- 1/4 teaspoon salt
- 2 cups pecan halves

Instructions:

1. Prepare the Pie Crust:

- In a large mixing bowl, combine the flour and salt. Add the chilled cubed butter.
- Use a pastry cutter or fork to cut the butter into the flour mixture until it resembles coarse crumbs.
- Gradually add the ice water, 1 tablespoon at a time, mixing with a fork, until the dough starts to come together.
- Gather the dough into a ball, flatten into a disk, wrap in plastic wrap, and refrigerate for at least 1 hour.

2. Roll Out and Line the Pie Pan:

- Preheat your oven to 375°F (190°C).

- On a lightly floured surface, roll out the chilled dough into a circle about 12 inches in diameter. Carefully transfer the dough to a 9-inch pie dish. Trim and crimp the edges as desired. Place the pie dish in the refrigerator while you prepare the filling.

3. Make the Filling:

- In a medium mixing bowl, whisk together the maple syrup, brown sugar, melted butter, beaten eggs, vanilla extract, and salt until well combined.
- Stir in the pecan halves, ensuring they are evenly coated with the maple syrup mixture.

4. Assemble and Bake the Pie:

- Pour the pecan filling into the prepared pie crust, spreading it out evenly.
- Place the pie on a baking sheet to catch any spills during baking.
- Bake in the preheated oven for 40-50 minutes, or until the filling is set and the crust is golden brown. If the edges of the crust start to brown too quickly, cover them with foil or a pie crust shield.

5. Cool and Serve:

- Remove the maple pecan pie from the oven and let it cool completely on a wire rack before serving.

6. Enjoy:

- Serve slices of homemade maple pecan pie at room temperature or slightly warmed, topped with whipped cream or vanilla ice cream if desired.

Tips:

- If you prefer a deeper maple flavor, you can substitute some or all of the brown sugar with maple sugar.
- Toasting the pecans before adding them to the filling can enhance their flavor. Simply spread the pecan halves on a baking sheet and bake in a preheated 350°F (175°C) oven for about 8-10 minutes, or until fragrant and lightly toasted.

- Store any leftover maple pecan pie in the refrigerator, covered, for up to 3-4 days. Serve chilled or bring to room temperature before serving.

This homemade maple pecan pie is rich, sweet, and nutty—a perfect dessert for autumn and holiday gatherings. Enjoy the wonderful flavors of maple and pecans in every delicious bite!

Spiced Apple Pie

Ingredients:

For the Pie Crust:

- 2 1/2 cups all-purpose flour
- 1 teaspoon salt
- 1 tablespoon granulated sugar
- 1 cup (2 sticks) cold unsalted butter, cut into small cubes
- 6-8 tablespoons ice water

For the Apple Filling:

- 6-7 medium-sized apples (a mix of tart and sweet varieties like Granny Smith and Honeycrisp), peeled, cored, and thinly sliced
- 1/2 cup granulated sugar
- 1/4 cup packed light brown sugar
- 2 tablespoons all-purpose flour
- 1 teaspoon ground cinnamon
- 1/4 teaspoon ground nutmeg
- 1/4 teaspoon ground cloves
- 1/4 teaspoon salt
- 1 tablespoon fresh lemon juice

For Assembly:

- 2 tablespoons unsalted butter, cut into small pieces
- 1 egg, beaten (for egg wash)
- Granulated sugar, for sprinkling on top

Instructions:

1. Make the Pie Crust:

- In a large mixing bowl, whisk together the flour, salt, and sugar.

- Add the cold cubed butter to the flour mixture. Use a pastry cutter or fork to cut the butter into the flour until the mixture resembles coarse crumbs.
- Gradually add the ice water, 1 tablespoon at a time, mixing with a fork, until the dough begins to come together.
- Divide the dough into two equal portions, shape each into a disk, wrap in plastic wrap, and refrigerate for at least 1 hour or overnight.

2. Prepare the Apple Filling:

- In a large bowl, combine the sliced apples, granulated sugar, brown sugar, flour, cinnamon, nutmeg, cloves, salt, and lemon juice. Toss until the apples are evenly coated.

3. Preheat Oven and Roll Out Pie Crust:

- Preheat your oven to 375°F (190°C).
- On a lightly floured surface, roll out one disk of chilled pie dough into a circle about 12 inches in diameter. Carefully transfer the dough to a 9-inch pie dish. Trim the edges if necessary, leaving about a 1-inch overhang.

4. Fill the Pie:

- Spoon the apple filling into the prepared pie crust, mounding the apples slightly in the center. Dot the top with small pieces of butter.

5. Roll Out and Arrange the Top Crust:

- Roll out the second disk of chilled pie dough into a circle about 12 inches in diameter.
- Carefully place the rolled-out dough over the filled pie. Trim any excess dough and crimp the edges to seal the top and bottom crusts together. Cut slits in the top crust to allow steam to escape during baking.

6. Egg Wash and Bake:

- Brush the top crust with beaten egg and sprinkle with granulated sugar for a golden, crispy finish.

- Place the pie on a baking sheet to catch any drips, and bake in the preheated oven for 45-55 minutes, or until the crust is golden brown and the filling is bubbling.

7. Cool and Serve:

- Allow the spiced apple pie to cool completely on a wire rack before slicing and serving.

8. Enjoy:

- Serve slices of homemade spiced apple pie warm or at room temperature, topped with a scoop of vanilla ice cream or a dollop of whipped cream if desired.

Tips:

- For the best texture and flavor, use a mix of tart and sweet apples such as Granny Smith, Honeycrisp, or Braeburn.
- If the edges of the pie crust start to brown too quickly during baking, cover them with foil or a pie crust shield to prevent burning.
- Store any leftover spiced apple pie covered at room temperature for up to 2 days, or refrigerate for longer storage. Reheat slices in the microwave or oven before serving.

This homemade spiced apple pie is a comforting and delicious dessert that's perfect for sharing with family and friends during the fall and holiday season. Enjoy the warm flavors of cinnamon, nutmeg, and cloves in every bite!

Peppermint Mocha Cupcakes

Ingredients:

For the Cupcakes:

- 1 1/4 cups all-purpose flour
- 1/2 cup unsweetened cocoa powder
- 1 teaspoon baking powder
- 1/2 teaspoon baking soda
- 1/4 teaspoon salt
- 1/2 cup strong brewed coffee, cooled to room temperature
- 1/2 cup buttermilk, at room temperature
- 1 teaspoon vanilla extract
- 1/2 cup (1 stick) unsalted butter, softened
- 1 cup granulated sugar
- 2 large eggs, at room temperature
- 1/4 teaspoon peppermint extract

For the Peppermint Frosting:

- 1 cup (2 sticks) unsalted butter, softened
- 4 cups powdered sugar
- 1/4 cup heavy cream or milk
- 1/2 teaspoon peppermint extract
- Crushed candy canes or peppermint candies, for garnish

Instructions:

1. Preheat Oven and Prepare Cupcake Pan:

- Preheat your oven to 350°F (175°C). Line a standard 12-cup muffin pan with cupcake liners.

2. Mix Dry Ingredients:

- In a medium bowl, whisk together the flour, cocoa powder, baking powder, baking soda, and salt. Set aside.

3. Prepare Coffee and Buttermilk:

- Brew a strong cup of coffee and let it cool to room temperature.
- In a separate bowl or measuring cup, combine the room temperature buttermilk and vanilla extract. Set aside.

4. Make Cupcake Batter:

- In a large mixing bowl, cream together the softened butter and granulated sugar until light and fluffy.
- Add the eggs, one at a time, mixing well after each addition.
- Stir in the peppermint extract.
- Gradually add the dry flour mixture to the butter mixture, alternating with the brewed coffee and buttermilk mixture, beginning and ending with the dry ingredients. Mix until just combined.

5. Fill Cupcake Liners:

- Divide the cupcake batter evenly among the prepared cupcake liners, filling each about 2/3 full.

6. Bake the Cupcakes:

- Bake in the preheated oven for 18-20 minutes, or until a toothpick inserted into the center of a cupcake comes out clean.
- Remove the cupcakes from the oven and let them cool in the pan for a few minutes before transferring them to a wire rack to cool completely.

7. Make Peppermint Frosting:

- In a large mixing bowl, beat the softened butter until smooth and creamy.
- Gradually add the powdered sugar, alternating with the heavy cream or milk, until the desired consistency is reached. Add more or less powdered sugar as needed.
- Stir in the peppermint extract until well combined.

8. Frost and Garnish Cupcakes:

- Once the cupcakes are completely cooled, pipe or spread the peppermint frosting onto the cupcakes using a piping bag or offset spatula.
- Sprinkle crushed candy canes or peppermint candies on top of the frosted cupcakes for a festive garnish.

9. Serve and Enjoy:

- Serve these delicious homemade peppermint mocha cupcakes at room temperature and enjoy the delightful combination of chocolate, espresso, and peppermint flavors.

Tips:

- For an extra mocha flavor, you can add 1-2 tablespoons of instant espresso powder to the cupcake batter along with the dry ingredients.
- Store leftover cupcakes in an airtight container in the refrigerator for up to 3-4 days. Bring them to room temperature before serving for the best taste and texture.

These peppermint mocha cupcakes are sure to be a hit at holiday parties or as a special treat during the winter season. Enjoy the festive flavors and delightful presentation of these homemade cupcakes!

Caramel Apple Tart

Ingredients:

For the Tart Crust:

- 1 1/4 cups all-purpose flour
- 1/4 cup granulated sugar
- 1/2 teaspoon salt
- 1/2 cup unsalted butter, cold and cut into small cubes
- 1 large egg yolk
- 2 tablespoons ice water

For the Caramel Apple Filling:

- 4-5 medium apples (such as Granny Smith), peeled, cored, and thinly sliced
- 1/2 cup granulated sugar
- 1/4 cup unsalted butter
- 1/4 cup heavy cream
- 1/2 teaspoon vanilla extract
- Pinch of salt

Instructions:

1. Make the Tart Crust:

- In a food processor, combine the flour, sugar, and salt. Pulse a few times to mix.
- Add the cold butter cubes and pulse until the mixture resembles coarse crumbs.
- In a small bowl, whisk together the egg yolk and ice water. With the food processor running, gradually add the egg mixture until the dough comes together.
- Turn the dough out onto a lightly floured surface and shape it into a disk. Wrap in plastic wrap and refrigerate for at least 1 hour.

2. Preheat Oven and Prepare Tart Pan:

- Preheat your oven to 375°F (190°C). Lightly grease a 9-inch tart pan with a removable bottom.

3. Roll Out and Line the Tart Pan:

- On a lightly floured surface, roll out the chilled dough into a circle slightly larger than your tart pan.
- Carefully transfer the rolled-out dough to the tart pan. Press the dough into the bottom and up the sides of the pan. Trim off any excess dough.

4. Prepare the Caramel Apple Filling:

- In a large skillet or saucepan, heat the granulated sugar over medium heat. Stir constantly until the sugar melts and turns golden brown.
- Carefully add the butter and stir until melted and combined with the caramelized sugar.
- Slowly pour in the heavy cream while stirring constantly. Be careful as the mixture will bubble up.
- Stir in the vanilla extract and a pinch of salt. Remove the caramel sauce from heat and let it cool slightly.
- Arrange the sliced apples in the prepared tart crust, overlapping them slightly.
- Pour the warm caramel sauce evenly over the arranged apples.

6. Bake the Tart:

- Place the tart pan on a baking sheet to catch any drips. Bake in the preheated oven for 30-35 minutes, or until the apples are tender and the crust is golden brown.

7. Cool and Serve:

- Allow the caramel apple tart to cool in the pan for at least 20-30 minutes before removing it from the tart pan.
- Serve slices of the caramel apple tart warm or at room temperature. Enjoy with a scoop of vanilla ice cream or a dollop of whipped cream, if desired.

Tips:

- For added flavor, you can sprinkle ground cinnamon or nutmeg over the apple slices before adding the caramel sauce.

- Store any leftover caramel apple tart in the refrigerator, covered, for up to 2-3 days. Reheat individual slices in the microwave before serving.

This homemade caramel apple tart is a wonderful dessert to enjoy during the fall season or any time you're craving a deliciously sweet and fruity treat. The combination of caramel, apples, and buttery crust is simply irresistible!

White Chocolate Peppermint Fudge

Ingredients:

- 3 cups white chocolate chips
- 1 (14-ounce) can sweetened condensed milk
- 1/2 teaspoon peppermint extract
- 1/2 cup crushed peppermint candies or candy canes
- Red or green food coloring (optional, for swirl effect)

Instructions:

1. Prepare the Pan:

- Line an 8x8-inch baking dish with parchment paper or aluminum foil, leaving some overhang for easy removal of the fudge later. Lightly grease the lined pan with cooking spray or butter.

2. Melt the White Chocolate:

- In a medium saucepan or microwave-safe bowl, combine the white chocolate chips and sweetened condensed milk.
- If using the stovetop, heat over low heat, stirring constantly, until the white chocolate is melted and the mixture is smooth.
- If using the microwave, heat in 30-second intervals, stirring in between each interval, until the white chocolate is melted and smooth.

3. Add Peppermint Flavor:

- Stir in the peppermint extract into the melted white chocolate mixture until well combined.

4. Add Crushed Peppermint:

- Fold in about 1/4 cup of the crushed peppermint candies or candy canes into the fudge mixture, reserving the rest for topping.

5. Pour and Swirl (Optional):

- Pour the white chocolate peppermint fudge mixture into the prepared baking dish, spreading it out evenly with a spatula.
- If desired, add a few drops of red or green food coloring to the top of the fudge. Use a toothpick or skewer to swirl the food coloring into the fudge for a festive marbled effect.

6. Add Toppings:

- Sprinkle the remaining crushed peppermint candies or candy canes evenly over the top of the fudge, pressing them gently into the surface.

7. Chill and Set:

- Place the fudge in the refrigerator for at least 2-3 hours, or until firm and set.

8. Cut and Serve:

- Once the fudge is completely set, remove it from the baking dish using the parchment paper or foil overhang.
- Use a sharp knife to cut the fudge into small squares.

9. Enjoy:

- Serve the homemade white chocolate peppermint fudge at room temperature or slightly chilled.

Tips:

- For a more intense peppermint flavor, you can add a little more peppermint extract to taste.
- Customize the fudge with different toppings such as white chocolate drizzle or additional crushed peppermint candies.
- Store leftover fudge in an airtight container in the refrigerator for up to 1-2 weeks. Bring it to room temperature before serving.

This white chocolate peppermint fudge is a delightful holiday treat that's sure to be a hit with family and friends. Enjoy the creamy texture and refreshing peppermint flavor in every bite!

Ginger Snaps

Ingredients:

- 2 cups all-purpose flour
- 2 teaspoons ground ginger
- 1 teaspoon ground cinnamon
- 1/4 teaspoon ground cloves
- 1 teaspoon baking soda
- 1/4 teaspoon salt
- 3/4 cup unsalted butter, softened
- 1 cup granulated sugar, plus extra for rolling
- 1 large egg
- 1/4 cup molasses
- 1 teaspoon vanilla extract

Instructions:

1. Preheat Oven:

- Preheat your oven to 350°F (175°C). Line baking sheets with parchment paper or silicone baking mats.

2. Mix Dry Ingredients:

- In a medium bowl, whisk together the flour, ground ginger, cinnamon, cloves, baking soda, and salt. Set aside.

3. Cream Butter and Sugar:

- In a large mixing bowl, beat the softened butter and sugar together until light and fluffy, about 2-3 minutes.

4. Add Wet Ingredients:

- Add the egg, molasses, and vanilla extract to the butter-sugar mixture. Beat until well combined.

5. Combine Wet and Dry Ingredients:

- Gradually add the dry ingredients to the wet ingredients, mixing until the dough comes together. The dough will be thick and slightly sticky.

6. Shape Dough into Balls:

- Scoop tablespoon-sized portions of dough and roll them into balls using your hands.

7. Roll Dough Balls in Sugar:

- Roll each dough ball in granulated sugar to coat completely.

8. Place on Baking Sheets:

- Arrange the sugar-coated dough balls on the prepared baking sheets, spacing them about 2 inches apart.

9. Bake:

- Bake in the preheated oven for 10-12 minutes, or until the cookies are set and slightly cracked on top.

10. Cool and Enjoy:

- Allow the cookies to cool on the baking sheets for a few minutes, then transfer them to a wire rack to cool completely.

11. Store:

- Store the gingersnap cookies in an airtight container at room temperature. They will keep well for several days.

Tips:

- For chewier cookies, slightly underbake them by removing them from the oven when they are still slightly soft in the center.
- You can adjust the spice levels by adding more or less ground ginger, cinnamon, or cloves to suit your taste preferences.
- Gingersnap cookies can be enjoyed on their own or paired with a cup of tea or coffee.

These homemade gingersnap cookies are perfect for holiday gatherings or as a sweet treat any time of the year. Enjoy the warm and spicy flavors of these delightful cookies!

Chocolate-Dipped Madeleines

Ingredients:

For the Madeleines:

- 2/3 cup (150g) unsalted butter, melted and cooled, plus extra for greasing the madeleine molds
- 3 large eggs
- 1/2 cup (100g) granulated sugar
- 1 teaspoon vanilla extract
- 1 cup (125g) all-purpose flour
- 1/2 teaspoon baking powder
- Pinch of salt
- Zest of 1 lemon (optional)

For Dipping:

- 8 ounces (225g) semi-sweet or dark chocolate, chopped
- 1 tablespoon unsalted butter
- Optional toppings: chopped nuts, sprinkles, or sea salt

Instructions:

1. Prepare the Madeleine Batter:

- Preheat your oven to 375°F (190°C). Generously butter madeleine molds or use a non-stick madeleine pan.
- In a mixing bowl, whisk together the eggs, sugar, and vanilla extract until pale and slightly thickened, about 2-3 minutes.
- Add the melted butter and mix until combined.
- In a separate bowl, sift together the flour, baking powder, and salt. Gradually add the dry ingredients to the wet ingredients, mixing until just combined.
- If using, fold in the lemon zest.

2. Fill the Madeleine Molds:

- Spoon the madeleine batter into the prepared molds, filling each mold about 3/4 full.

3. Bake the Madeleines:

- Bake in the preheated oven for 10-12 minutes, or until the edges of the madeleines are golden brown and the tops spring back when lightly touched.
- Remove the madeleines from the oven and let them cool in the pan for a few minutes before transferring them to a wire rack to cool completely.

4. Prepare the Chocolate Coating:

- In a microwave-safe bowl or using a double boiler, melt the chopped chocolate and tablespoon of butter together until smooth and glossy.

5. Dip the Madeleines:

- Dip each cooled madeleine halfway into the melted chocolate, allowing any excess chocolate to drip off.
- Place the dipped madeleines on a parchment-lined baking sheet.

6. Add Toppings (Optional):

- While the chocolate is still wet, sprinkle chopped nuts, sprinkles, or a pinch of sea salt on top of the dipped madeleines for decoration.

7. Let the Chocolate Set:

- Allow the chocolate-dipped madeleines to set at room temperature or place them in the refrigerator for quicker setting.

8. Serve and Enjoy:

- Serve the chocolate-dipped madeleines as a delightful dessert or sweet treat with tea or coffee.

Tips:

- Ensure the madeleine pan is well-greased to prevent sticking.
- For added flavor, you can use orange zest instead of lemon zest in the madeleine batter.
- Experiment with different types of chocolate for dipping, such as milk chocolate or white chocolate, for variety.

- Store the chocolate-dipped madeleines in an airtight container at room temperature for a few days. Enjoy them within a couple of days for the best taste and texture.

These homemade chocolate-dipped madeleines are sure to impress with their elegant appearance and delicious flavor. Enjoy the combination of buttery madeleines and rich, decadent chocolate!

Pistachio Cranberry Biscotti

Ingredients:

- 2 cups all-purpose flour
- 1 cup granulated sugar
- 1 teaspoon baking powder
- 1/2 teaspoon salt
- 3 large eggs
- 1 teaspoon vanilla extract
- Zest of 1 orange
- 1 cup shelled pistachios, roughly chopped
- 1 cup dried cranberries

Instructions:

1. Preheat Oven:

    - Preheat your oven to 350°F (175°C). Line a baking sheet with parchment paper or a silicone baking mat.

2. Mix Dry Ingredients:

    - In a large mixing bowl, whisk together the flour, sugar, baking powder, and salt.

3. Prepare Wet Ingredients:

    - In a separate bowl, whisk together the eggs, vanilla extract, and orange zest until well combined.

4. Combine Wet and Dry Ingredients:

    - Gradually add the wet ingredients to the dry ingredients, mixing until a dough forms.

5. Add Pistachios and Cranberries:

- Fold in the chopped pistachios and dried cranberries until evenly distributed in the dough.

6. Shape the Dough:

- Divide the dough in half. On a lightly floured surface, shape each half of the dough into a log about 12 inches long and 2 inches wide. Place the logs on the prepared baking sheet, spacing them a few inches apart.

7. Bake the Biscotti Logs:

- Bake in the preheated oven for 25-30 minutes, or until the logs are firm to the touch and lightly golden.

8. Cool and Slice:

- Remove the biscotti logs from the oven and let them cool on the baking sheet for 10-15 minutes.
- Using a serrated knife, carefully slice the logs diagonally into 1/2-inch thick slices.

9. Bake Again:

- Arrange the biscotti slices cut-side down on the baking sheet. Bake for an additional 10-12 minutes, flipping the biscotti halfway through baking, until they are crisp and golden brown.

10. Cool and Serve:

- Let the pistachio cranberry biscotti cool completely on a wire rack before serving.

11. Enjoy:

- Serve the homemade biscotti with coffee, tea, or dessert wine for dipping and enjoy the delightful combination of pistachios, cranberries, and orange zest.

Tips:

- For an extra festive touch, drizzle melted white or dark chocolate over the cooled biscotti.
- Store the biscotti in an airtight container at room temperature for up to two weeks. They also freeze well for longer storage.

These homemade pistachio cranberry biscotti make a wonderful holiday gift or a delightful treat to enjoy any time of the year. Enjoy the crunchy texture and delicious flavors of these Italian cookies!

Nutella Swirl Bread

Ingredients:

- 2 1/4 teaspoons (1 packet) active dry yeast
- 1 cup warm milk (about 110°F or 43°C)
- 1/4 cup granulated sugar
- 1/3 cup unsalted butter, melted and cooled
- 1 teaspoon vanilla extract
- 3 1/2 cups all-purpose flour
- 1/2 teaspoon salt
- 1/2 cup Nutella (or other chocolate-hazelnut spread)
- 1 egg, beaten (for egg wash)
- Optional: powdered sugar, for dusting

Instructions:

1. Activate the Yeast:

- In a small bowl, dissolve the yeast in the warm milk. Let it sit for 5-10 minutes until frothy.

2. Mix Dough:

- In a large mixing bowl or the bowl of a stand mixer fitted with a dough hook, combine the activated yeast mixture, sugar, melted butter, and vanilla extract.
- Gradually add the flour and salt, mixing until a soft dough forms.

3. Knead the Dough:

- Knead the dough by hand on a floured surface or using a stand mixer with the dough hook attachment, until the dough is smooth and elastic, about 5-7 minutes.

4. First Rise:

- Place the dough in a greased bowl, turning once to coat the dough with oil. Cover with a clean kitchen towel or plastic wrap and let it rise in a warm place until doubled in size, about 1-2 hours.

5. Prepare Loaf:

    - Punch down the risen dough and turn it out onto a lightly floured surface.
    - Roll the dough out into a rectangle, about 12x18 inches in size.

6. Add Nutella Swirl:

    - Spread the Nutella evenly over the surface of the dough, leaving a small border around the edges.

7. Roll and Shape:

    - Starting from one of the longer sides, tightly roll up the dough into a log.
    - Pinch the seams to seal and place the dough seam-side down in a greased 9x5-inch loaf pan.

8. Second Rise:

    - Cover the loaf pan with a clean kitchen towel or plastic wrap and let it rise in a warm place for another 30-45 minutes, until the dough rises slightly above the rim of the pan.

9. Preheat Oven:

    - Meanwhile, preheat your oven to 350°F (175°C).

10. Brush with Egg Wash:

    - Brush the top of the risen loaf with beaten egg, which will give it a shiny finish when baked.

11. Bake:

- Bake the Nutella swirl bread in the preheated oven for 30-35 minutes, or until the top is golden brown and the bread sounds hollow when tapped on the bottom.

12. Cool and Serve:

- Allow the bread to cool in the pan for 10-15 minutes, then transfer it to a wire rack to cool completely.

13. Optional: Dust with Powdered Sugar:

- Once cooled, you can dust the Nutella swirl bread with powdered sugar for a decorative touch.

14. Slice and Enjoy:

- Slice the Nutella swirl bread and enjoy it warm or at room temperature. It's delicious on its own or toasted with a spread of butter.

Tips:

- Make sure your Nutella is at room temperature for easier spreading.
- You can customize this recipe by adding chopped nuts, chocolate chips, or a sprinkle of sea salt to the Nutella filling before rolling up the dough.
- Store any leftover Nutella swirl bread in an airtight container at room temperature for up to 3-4 days. It can also be frozen for longer storage.

This homemade Nutella swirl bread is a wonderful treat that's sure to be enjoyed by chocolate lovers of all ages. Enjoy the soft, fluffy bread with swirls of creamy Nutella in every bite!

Eggnog Bread Pudding

Ingredients:

- 2 1/4 teaspoons (1 packet) active dry yeast
- 1 cup warm milk (about 110°F or 43°C)
- 1/4 cup granulated sugar
- 1/3 cup unsalted butter, melted and cooled
- 1 teaspoon vanilla extract
- 3 1/2 cups all-purpose flour
- 1/2 teaspoon salt
- 1/2 cup Nutella (or other chocolate-hazelnut spread)
- 1 egg, beaten (for egg wash)
- Optional: powdered sugar, for dusting

Instructions:

1. Activate the Yeast:

- In a small bowl, dissolve the yeast in the warm milk. Let it sit for 5-10 minutes until frothy.

2. Mix Dough:

- In a large mixing bowl or the bowl of a stand mixer fitted with a dough hook, combine the activated yeast mixture, sugar, melted butter, and vanilla extract.
- Gradually add the flour and salt, mixing until a soft dough forms.

3. Knead the Dough:

- Knead the dough by hand on a floured surface or using a stand mixer with the dough hook attachment, until the dough is smooth and elastic, about 5-7 minutes.

4. First Rise:

- Place the dough in a greased bowl, turning once to coat the dough with oil. Cover with a clean kitchen towel or plastic wrap and let it rise in a warm place until doubled in size, about 1-2 hours.

5. Prepare Loaf:

    - Punch down the risen dough and turn it out onto a lightly floured surface.
    - Roll the dough out into a rectangle, about 12x18 inches in size.

6. Add Nutella Swirl:

    - Spread the Nutella evenly over the surface of the dough, leaving a small border around the edges.

7. Roll and Shape:

    - Starting from one of the longer sides, tightly roll up the dough into a log.
    - Pinch the seams to seal and place the dough seam-side down in a greased 9x5-inch loaf pan.

8. Second Rise:

    - Cover the loaf pan with a clean kitchen towel or plastic wrap and let it rise in a warm place for another 30-45 minutes, until the dough rises slightly above the rim of the pan.

9. Preheat Oven:

    - Meanwhile, preheat your oven to 350°F (175°C).

10. Brush with Egg Wash:

    - Brush the top of the risen loaf with beaten egg, which will give it a shiny finish when baked.

11. Bake:

- Bake the Nutella swirl bread in the preheated oven for 30-35 minutes, or until the top is golden brown and the bread sounds hollow when tapped on the bottom.

12. Cool and Serve:

- Allow the bread to cool in the pan for 10-15 minutes, then transfer it to a wire rack to cool completely.

13. Optional: Dust with Powdered Sugar:

- Once cooled, you can dust the Nutella swirl bread with powdered sugar for a decorative touch.

14. Slice and Enjoy:

- Slice the Nutella swirl bread and enjoy it warm or at room temperature. It's delicious on its own or toasted with a spread of butter.

Tips:

- Make sure your Nutella is at room temperature for easier spreading.
- You can customize this recipe by adding chopped nuts, chocolate chips, or a sprinkle of sea salt to the Nutella filling before rolling up the dough.
- Store any leftover Nutella swirl bread in an airtight container at room temperature for up to 3-4 days. It can also be frozen for longer storage.

This homemade Nutella swirl bread is a wonderful treat that's sure to be enjoyed by chocolate lovers of all ages. Enjoy the soft, fluffy bread with swirls of creamy Nutella in every bite!

Eggnog Bread Pudding

Eggnog bread pudding is a delightful and comforting dessert, perfect for the holiday season. This recipe combines rich eggnog with bread cubes, eggs, and warm spices to create a decadent and flavorful treat. Here's how to make homemade eggnog bread pudding:

Ingredients:

- 6 cups day-old bread, such as French bread or brioche, cut into cubes
- 2 cups eggnog
- 3 large eggs
- 1/2 cup granulated sugar
- 1 teaspoon vanilla extract
- 1/2 teaspoon ground nutmeg
- 1/4 teaspoon ground cinnamon
- 1/4 teaspoon salt
- 1/2 cup raisins or dried cranberries (optional)
- Powdered sugar, for dusting (optional)
- Whipped cream or vanilla ice cream, for serving (optional)

Instructions:

1. Preheat Oven:

- Preheat your oven to 350°F (175°C). Grease a 9x9-inch baking dish with butter or non-stick cooking spray.

2. Prepare Bread Cubes:

- Place the bread cubes in the prepared baking dish.

3. Make Eggnog Custard Mixture:

- In a mixing bowl, whisk together the eggnog, eggs, granulated sugar, vanilla extract, nutmeg, cinnamon, and salt until well combined.

4. Pour Custard Over Bread:

- Pour the eggnog custard mixture evenly over the bread cubes in the baking dish. Gently press down on the bread to ensure all pieces are soaked in the custard.

5. Add Optional Raisins or Cranberries:

- Sprinkle raisins or dried cranberries over the top of the bread pudding, if using.

6. Bake:

- Place the baking dish in the preheated oven and bake for 35-40 minutes, or until the bread pudding is set and golden brown on top.

7. Cool Slightly:

- Remove the bread pudding from the oven and let it cool slightly for 10-15 minutes before serving.

8. Serve:

- Serve the eggnog bread pudding warm, dusted with powdered sugar if desired, and topped with whipped cream or vanilla ice cream.

9. Enjoy:

- Enjoy this delicious eggnog bread pudding as a festive dessert for holiday gatherings or special occasions.

Tips:

- Use a good-quality eggnog for the best flavor. You can use store-bought eggnog or make your own homemade eggnog.
- Feel free to customize the bread pudding by adding chopped nuts, chocolate chips, or other dried fruits along with the bread cubes.

- Leftover bread pudding can be stored in the refrigerator for up to 3-4 days. Reheat individual servings in the microwave or oven before serving.

This eggnog bread pudding is a wonderful way to enjoy the flavors of the season in a comforting and satisfying dessert. It's sure to become a holiday favorite for family and friends!

Sparkling Cranberry Orange Cookies

Ingredients:

- 1 cup dried cranberries
- Zest of 1 large orange
- 1 cup unsalted butter, softened
- 1 cup granulated sugar
- 1/2 cup brown sugar, packed
- 2 large eggs
- 1 teaspoon vanilla extract
- 3 cups all-purpose flour
- 1 teaspoon baking soda
- 1/2 teaspoon salt
- 1/2 cup coarse sugar or granulated sugar (for rolling)

Instructions:

1. Preheat Oven:

   - Preheat your oven to 350°F (175°C). Line baking sheets with parchment paper or silicone baking mats.

2. Prepare Cranberries:

   - In a small bowl, combine the dried cranberries with the orange zest. Toss to coat the cranberries with the zest and set aside.

3. Cream Butter and Sugars:

   - In a large mixing bowl, cream together the softened butter, granulated sugar, and brown sugar until light and fluffy.

4. Add Eggs and Vanilla:

   - Beat in the eggs, one at a time, until well combined. Mix in the vanilla extract.

5. Mix Dry Ingredients:

- In a separate bowl, whisk together the flour, baking soda, and salt.

6. Combine Wet and Dry Ingredients:

- Gradually add the dry ingredients to the wet ingredients, mixing until just combined.

7. Fold in Cranberries and Orange Zest:

- Gently fold in the cranberries and orange zest until evenly distributed throughout the cookie dough.

8. Roll Dough into Balls:

- Scoop tablespoon-sized portions of dough and roll them into balls using your hands.

9. Roll in Sugar:

- Roll each dough ball in coarse sugar or granulated sugar to coat completely.

10. Place on Baking Sheets:

- Arrange the sugar-coated dough balls on the prepared baking sheets, spacing them about 2 inches apart.

11. Bake:

- Bake in the preheated oven for 10-12 minutes, or until the edges of the cookies are golden brown.

12. Cool and Enjoy:

- Allow the cookies to cool on the baking sheets for a few minutes, then transfer them to a wire rack to cool completely.

13. Serve:

- Serve these sparkling cranberry orange cookies as a delightful holiday treat with a cup of tea or coffee.

Tips:

- Make sure your butter is softened but not melted for the best cookie texture.
- You can substitute fresh cranberries for dried cranberries if desired, but be aware that fresh cranberries will add more tartness to the cookies.
- Store leftover cookies in an airtight container at room temperature for up to one week. Enjoy them as a festive snack or dessert!

These sparkling cranberry orange cookies are sure to be a hit with their festive appearance and delicious flavor. Enjoy the combination of cranberries and orange zest in every bite!